SELECTING AND MANAGING ELECTRONIC RESOURCES

Z
292

A How-To-Do-It Manual

Vicki L. Gregory

HOW-TO-DO-IT MANUALS FOR LIBRARIANS

NUMBER 101

NEAL-SCHUMAN PUBLISHERS, INC.
New York, London

Published by Neal-Schuman Publishers, Inc.
100 Varick Street
New York, NY 10013

The paper used in this publication meets the minimum requirements of American National Standard for Information Sciences—Permanence of Paper for Printed Library Materials, ANSI Z39.48–1992.

Printed and bound in the United States of America.

ISBN 1–55570–382–8

Library of Congress Cataloging-in-Publication Data

Gregory, Vicki L., 1950–
  Selecting and managing electronic resources: a how-to-do-it manual for librarians / Vicki L. Gregory.
    p.   cm. — (How-to-do-it manuals for librarians ; no. 101)
  Includes bibliographical references (p.).
  ISBN 1-55570-382-8 (alk. paper)
    1. Libraries—United States—Special collections—Electronic information resources. 2. Libraries—United States—Special collections—Databases. 3. Database selection. 4. Cataloging of computer files—United States. 5. Cataloging of databases—United States. I. Title. II. How-to-do-it manuals for libraries ; no. 101.

Z692.D38 G74 2000
                                        00-041569

CONTENTS

LIST OF FIGURES

1 INTRODUCTION

Building a library collection has always been a process requiring tolerance of continuous change and the need for evaluation and reevaluation. Over the years, most libraries have evolved fairly standard processes for collecting print collections and later adding audiovisual materials to the print mix. But these standard processes necessarily had to evolve as conditions, user needs, and resources changed. Today, the problem has altered once again. In order to keep up with the current needs of their users, libraries must now also include electronic resources in their collections and purchase and maintain the necessary hardware and software to make those resources available in the library. Further, more often than not, libraries are today also being called upon to provide the means for users to access library collections remotely from their home or office.

The growing user preference for electronic resources has severely affected the budgets of most libraries. These new resources do not replace existing materials and therefore they represent still another format that must be collected if the library is to keep up with the times. Unfortunately these new resources also require a somewhat different expertise for selection and evaluation. More than subject-matter expertise is needed to select these materials; the selector must also have technical expertise (or have access to those with technical expertise) in order to evaluate both what equipment may be needed to access the new product and how well the product performs.

Libraries used to be able to measure their resources in terms of feet (or miles) of shelf, but the extent of their collections is now more accurately measured in terms of a combination of the resources physically present in the library building and the level or degree of access that is provided to electronic resources. However, in most ways, collection development remains fundamentally the same in purpose—that is, a decision-making process for considering the information needs of users, for considering the value and extent of the existing library collection and available information resources, and for determining which resources will best meet the information needs of the library users and are therefore most suitable for addition to the collection. Thus, even in the electronic age, collection development librarians must still identify, locate, and organize materials so that patrons can find the information that they need or desire.

For roughly 15 years or more now, the library community has been discussing and writing about the imminent change from paper to purely electronic collections, leading many to believe that soon there would be no necessity for print resources because everything would be available only in the form of an electronic publication. Although the so-called "paperless society" has failed to materialize in other than certain very narrow areas, library collections and the clients of virtually all libraries have nevertheless become more and more dependent on electronic resources. Initially, some librarians thought they could treat the new electronic resources as fads, and safely ignore the Internet and other electronic resources. For a good many years, this view did not present too much of a problem, as most of the population failed to learn or adapt very well to character-based computing. With the rise and predominance of the graphical user interface on the computer desktop, however, and when confronted with the overwhelming acceptance of the Web and the resultant expansion of computer literacy to a majority of the general population, a great deal of pressure has been placed on libraries to provide more electronic products and services, to the point that it is clearly no longer possible for electronic resources to be considered "optional" or luxuries. Indeed, they are fast becoming essential mainstays of every library's collection.

Today's electronic information arena involves resources covering a wide variety of materials, including indexing and abstracting services, electronic books and serials, electronic databases offered by information aggregators, document delivery services, and Web sites. Many of these resources may be locally mounted on a library's server, or they may be accessed remotely by modem or, increasingly, through direct Internet connections maintained by the library. The emergence of the Web as an important form of information delivery has provided a viable alternative to the acquisition of many resources that would traditionally have been locally owned and housed. The Web, through the many available Web browsers and search engines, has itself become a standardizing element that has stimulated a migration from print to electronic form for many publications. The Web as a real-time distribution channel has also solved many distribution and access problems by eliminating the need for vendors to develop and distribute proprietary software in order for clients to access their resources.

But while much on the Internet remains free, much that is free all too often suffers from a lack of depth, and vendors have come to realize that hard-copy sales may be replaced by the license approach. In the electronic arena, therefore, selection will continue to be one of the major issues in the provision of information. The process of selection is perhaps becoming more complex as a result (at least in the sense that, in addition to content, such factors as package deals for electronic resources come into play, and the entire process may therefore become more focused on groups of resources rather than being a title-by-title process), but selection is still key to the delivery of information services. As with print resources, there is a need to establish and apply appropriate criteria in order to determine systematically the quality and value of a particular electronic resource for a particular collection. How to do this best is the trick, and the inclusion of extensive electronic resources has so changed many library services and functions that, by necessity, many departmental barriers between the public and technical sides of the library must be broken down. This cross-functionality is the key and will be emphasized at length in this handbook.

Major steps, processes, and issues to be confronted in dealing with the incorporation of electronic resources into a library collection will also be discussed. Unfortunately, today there are still more questions than answers in many areas, but reviewing the issues involved will nevertheless be beneficial to librarians embarking on the integration of electronic resources into their existing print collections. Few universally "right" answers ever exist to many information access questions anyway, and when there appear to be several approaches to a particular issue, this book lays out alternatives to assist librarians in choosing the best solution for their library's situation.

Chapter 2 deals with those collection development policies that are either dedicated to electronic resources or that make adequate provisions for electronic resources. In the 1970s most libraries began establishing written collection development policies for what were basically print collections with some appended audiovisual materials. Today, electronic resources are becoming such an integral part of a library's resources, not just an added-on frill, that collection development policies need to be rewritten significantly or amended to take these electronic resources into account. An integrated collection development policy for all types of materials and formats is therefore advocated.

Chapter 3 opens with a discussion of needs assessment, that is, the determination of what electronic resources and what format of those resources will best meet the needs of the users of a particular library. Following needs assessment, selection criteria for electronic resources is discussed along with available selection tools for electronic resources. Selection criteria are important even for "free" Internet resources, since these criteria help to ensure that standards (intended to determine whether the resources are authoritative and trustworthy) have been applied, not just that the "cost" of the resource was right. New methods for selection, including trial offers, demonstrations, and visits to libraries already owning or licensing the particular electronic resource are then reviewed. Chapter 3 also covers how the selection process is best carried out and includes a discussion of the use of selection teams, which combine both subject and technical expertise for the selection and implementation of electronic information resources.

Chapter 4 deals with acquisitions and budgeting in the electronic resource era. The traditional primary skills of a selector have always been subject-matter knowledge and a knowledge of the publishing structure for the particular discipline involved. Now these skills must be augmented with knowledgeability concerning the technical aspects of the materials, the various copyright and licensing issues that those materials may suggest, and the roadmap of the various bundles of electronic materials (in order to best compare their respective coverages and prices). Because the work of a collection development librarian is made much more complex by the way many electronic resources are now sold in package deals, or purchased jointly or through consortial arrangements that greatly reduce the cost to individual libraries, a sampling of Web resources and vendors who supply bundles of electronic resources is provided.

Chapter 5 deals with the organization and maintenance of electronic resources, including the cataloging or other bibliographic control of electronic resources, as well as issues involved with the authentication of users. As with print resources, once an electronic information resource is selected, the library must provide some organized method of making its users aware of the resource and how to access it. After all, library users are not really concerned about whether a resource is owned locally or that access to it is provided from a remote server, as long as they can get to it and the cost for retrieval is the same. Therefore, electronic materials that have been selected by the library need to be organized or set up for easy retrieval by users. As part of the organization of electronic materials for patron access, authentication of users and the various ways in which licensing agreements with vendors allow for authentication are also discussed.

Chapter 6 deals with evaluation and assessment of electronic resources. Library professionals have generally thought of library assessments in terms of their book or serials collections only, but assessment and evaluation are equally important for electronic resources and in determining the effectiveness of a library's ideal mix of electronic and printed resources. Techniques for assessment are discussed and a number of areas where data are needed for a successful evaluation are pointed out.

Electronic resources have heightened libraries' concerns dealing with copyright and licensing for libraries. Chapter 7 looks at some of the issues arising from publishers' and vendors' concerns for their intellectual property rights in electronic products where copying and reproducing their work have been greatly simplified. Another important issue addressed in this chapter is ownership versus licensing of resources, with the implications for possible restrictions on the fair use rights of users. The emergence of the Uniform Computer Information Transactions Act (UCITA) and its potentially deleterious effect on libraries in regard to licensing issues is also discussed in this chapter.

The traditional preservation role of libraries also presents a number of new issues when electronic resources are concerned. Chapter 8 examines some of the most pressing concerns that libraries have for the preservation of and continued access to electronic materials. Many librarians lack sufficient confidence in the lifespan and continued availability of electronic materials to substitute them for print materials and they are continuing print subscriptions for items also being purchased in electronic format—an expensive and sometimes justified approach, but usually a clearly wasteful one. A corollary concern is media access through the hardware or software needed to access the material. Librarians who purchased 8-track audiotapes or film loops in the 1970s clearly understand how ownership of the actual media may not be worth much if it can no longer be used due to a lack of hardware that will play the tape or film. Most librarians also remember 8-inch and $5\frac{1}{4}$-inch floppy disks. Guarantees that the material will be updated or migrated to current operating systems and formats become important and problematic issues.

Selecting and managing electronic resources is a new area of concern for libraries and not one that was envisioned as a major issue when many of today's practicing librarians attended library school, but it is an area through which all librarians are having to find their way today, and in many ways blaze new trails. It is the purpose of this work to assist in cutting down some of the foliage and vines along the trail.

2 COLLECTION DEVELOPMENT POLICIES

Collection development policies are really best viewed as blueprints for the operations of a library as a whole, for it is through these policies that the library carries out its central tasks of acquiring, organizing, and maintaining library materials. Collection development policies also typically set up the general framework for establishing the library's collection goals, in terms of both new acquisitions and the maintenance of the existing items in the library's collections. Usually written and developed by libraries with two audiences in mind—the library's staff members and the broader community of the library's patrons and other users—collection development policies certainly vary greatly as a result. In most libraries, however, what we find today is a combination of descriptions of practices, guidelines for decisions, and provisions intended to protect against unwarranted pressures to acquire, to eschew the acquisition of, or to discard certain types of materials or particular items.

Collection development policies help to ensure consistency in procedures and are also important in achieving appropriate balance in the library's collection. This need for consistency exists because selectors, in using and revising the policies, are necessarily forced to confront the overall goals and objectives of the library and to reflect these goals and objectives in the collection they are building, whether that collection is owned and housed locally in hard copy form or in an electronic format or is simply accessed through the Web. Of course, proper collection balance does not mean that all areas must receive equal coverage, but rather that the collection reflect the proper balance necessary to meet the needs of the particular library's users. This touchstone remains as valid in the electronic arena as it has always been in the traditional print environment.

The rapid infusion into the stream of materials available for library acquisition of all manners and types of electronic resources (including electronic journals, databases, image collections, maps, encyclopedias, stock market reports, and other business and financial information) has, as might be expected, often strained the old rules and guidelines typically contained in traditional collection development policies. What constitutes the "library's collection"? Is it simply those items that are purchased and housed locally or does it include licensed materials that are housed on a server at the vendor's site? Does (or should) the collection include materials that are freely available on the Internet? These basic philosophical issues must be resolved before a successful collection development policy for electronic resources can be written today. Only once these issues are settled will the library be ready to write or revise its current policy to take electronic materials into account.

Three approaches to considering the acquisition or retention of electronic resources pursuant to libraries' collection development policies have typically been taken:

- Making electronic resources acquisitions fit into the patterns of traditional policies.
- Creating separate policies dealing only with electronic resources.
- Mainstreaming electronic resources into a reworked, integrated collection development policy.

As will be seen below, only the third approach is likely to be successful. Few today would doubt that electronic resources are here to stay in one form or another, and, as time goes on, these resources will doubtless come to represent a larger portion and more important component of a typical library's collection, both in terms of number of items and expenditures. For this, if no other reason, it is vital that electronic resources be included in the overall collection plans of any library and not ignored or simply addressed separately.

TRADITIONAL POLICIES

Traditional collection development policies have typically served a number of purposes, some of which have the effect of informing and directing library processes in acquiring and making resources available to users, and some of which have served as a protection for the library against challenges to its procedures and resources. These purposes—**informing**, **directing**, and **protecting**—can be accomplished or carried out in many ways through a traditional collection development policy. To carry out the **informing** and **directing** purposes, a traditional collection development policy typically contains provisions intended to:

- Describe the library's user community, defining the institutional mission of the library, and identifying its users' likely needs.
- Provide selection criteria and guidelines for the use of those charged with selecting library materials.
- Identify those selection tools and processes that are most appropriate for the particular library.
- Define the process for identifying materials for weeding, cancellation, storage, and replacement of materials.
- Facilitate consistency and communication among the library's collection development librarians.

- Establish who is responsible for various aspects of the collection development process and collection management activities.
- Create a plan for the future of the collection and the budgeting of resultant library expenditures.
- Serve as a training document for new collection development librarians and those charged with management of the library as a whole.
- Provide guidelines for dealing with gift materials.
- Provide guidelines for dealing with complaints about materials or services thought by patrons or administrators to be inappropriate.
- Provide a framework and context for decisions concerning library access, space allocations, budgeting, and fund-raising priorities.
- Support cooperative collection development activities by documenting what the library has done in the past and what the library is currently doing with collecting levels by discipline.
- Identify both the strengths and the relative weaknesses of the library's current collections.
- Aid in preparing grant proposals and planning development initiatives through its supporting documentation.
- Serve as a communication vehicle with the library's staff, administration, and its various constituencies.

A good collection development policy will carry out its **protecting** purposes by containing provisions in such areas as:

- Protecting intellectual freedom.
- Informing the library's governing and/or funding body concerning the library's current direction.
- Providing a clear and carefully described rationale for the library's collection goals and practices.
- Making clear the principles under which decisions are made to protect the library against charges of bias and irresponsible behavior.
- Protecting the library from pressures to acquire or provide access to inappropriate or irrelevant resources.
- Acting as an informational tool for use within the library's user/ patron community and for its community at large.
- Providing some protection to the library, when budgets decrease and/or materials costs increase, against complaints by the user community.

An examination of the purposes of the traditional library collection development policy reveals that virtually every one of the issues remains present and important, perhaps to a greater or lesser degree, when dealing with electronic resources. But a number of additional different and unique concerns do exist. A collection development policy that is intended to encompass electronic resources can successfully do so only if it seeks to address the issues of:

- Cancellation or retention of print resources when the electronic version of the resource becomes available.
- Provision of or limitations on remote access to electronic resources owned or licensed by the library.
- Justification of new costs, which may include the costs of hardware and supplies in addition to the cost of the material.
- Location of resources and the cost of maintaining appropriate Internet or other network links.
- Possible duplication of certain e-journals or databases, based on purchasing bundles available from different electronic information aggregators.
- Negotiation of the terms of licenses for use of the material, including provisions addressing these new types of legal considerations in the collection development policy itself.
- Consideration of the special preservation and long-term access issues that electronic resources present.
- Satisfaction by the library of the technical requirements for access to the resource, including such matters as determining the formats and computer platforms supported by the materials.
- Cancellation problems, which include whether the library loses all rights to materials previously licensed once cancellation occurs.
- Performance questions, such as whether the electronic product really performs its intended job better (that is, does it make information more easily or accurately available than its print counterpart?).
- Training of staff and users in the use of the particular new electronic resource.
- Access and organizational issues concerning whether to catalog Internet-available items or electronic bundles of resources.
- Cooperative collection development issues, such as the ability to provide copies on interlibrary loan.

These issues and others make it clear that a collection development policy written purely for or with only the print environment in mind will not be of much use in the selection and management of electronic resources. Therefore, hard as it may be to do so, the old policies are best discarded in favor of new approaches that keep the goals of those policies alive but reflect the realities of the electronic information environment.

SEPARATE POLICIES

When conventional collection development policies are perceived as having become inadequate in resolving the issues that typically revolve around electronic resources, many libraries have resorted to the development of a separate collection development policy specifically intended to cover the acquisition and maintenance of electronic resources. In some ways these "separate" policies are not that much different from the traditional approaches. For example, a separate policy might be developed for the selection of CD-ROM products; it might generally follow the basic philosophies of the library's traditional collection development policy, but supplement it by adding appropriate guidelines in respect of such matters as:

- Keeping the selection of CD-ROMs consistent with general collection development policies.
- Evaluating the searching and system capabilities (such as Boolean searching, response time, and downloading capability) of the CD-ROM product, in addition to evaluating its informational content.
- Evaluating CD-ROM vendors in terms of reliability and support as well as the validity of the informational content of their products.
- Determining the administrative costs associated with the CD-ROM product in addition to other related costs, such as those for hardware upgrades, additional disk space requirements, maintenance, and security.
- Evaluating the amount of instructional time required for staff and users to learn how to use the product effectively.
- Updating procedures, including new ones for determining whether years for the product are "rolled-off," thereby resulting in loss of coverage for earlier years.
- Networking requirements/costs for the CD-ROM product.

The separate policy approach can work, but usually only if the library has plans to obtain a limited amount of electronic information products. Thus, as more and more electronic products are purchased or licensed, the need for an integrated policy quickly becomes more apparent. First of all, if the policy is to work well, all of the library's collection development librarians will typically have to be involved to some extent in the selection of electronic resources. A separate policy approach that tends to label these resources as "special" or different from print resources at a time when a mix of electronic and print resources is fast becoming the norm throughout all areas in the library will quickly become inadequate. Also, to isolate the decisions regarding print and electronic resources is to beg for massive duplication. If the decision-making process is integrated, and it should be, it seems logical for the collection development policy to be an integrated one as well. On balance then, separate collection development policies for electronic resources should be avoided.

INTEGRATED POLICIES

Integrating electronic resources into the library's overall collection development policy has many advantages. Perhaps foremost among these advantages is that integration allows electronic resources to be placed into the plan for the overall goals of the library so that they may take their rightful place in the collection as an integral part of the library's materials in a given subject area. This process naturally leads to a unity of resources and avoids the potentially unfocused groupings of electronic materials at various "spots." This is particularly important for selectors who may otherwise miss or be generally unaware of important electronic resources within their respective specialties. Indeed, the role of the selectors remains critical, and the collection development policy should be designed first and foremost to help them do their jobs.

Important considerations for any integrated collection development policy include:

- Provisions allowing selectors to learn about and see which electronic resources would fill gaps in their library's current print collection.
- Provisions for the inclusion of prescriptive information regarding the various selection tools that review electronic resources (these tools might not initially be familiar to all selectors).
- Allowance for a more rational approach to funding the purchase of resources, both print and electronic, when viewed as a whole.
- Provision of help to library administrators and staff when challenged by users who may resist the inclusion in the collection of new and inherently expensive electronic resources.
- Allowance for more flexibility regarding new formats and types of resources.
- Encouragement of collection development across formats.

Of course, fully integrating electronic resources into a library's collection development policy means that selection criteria that pertain to electronic materials and discussion of issues particular, if not peculiar, to electronic resources must be added, wherever appropriate and needed, to the library's collection development policy. Some issues that will always need to be addressed or included in a properly integrated collection development policy are:

- Licensing issues, such as numbers of users allowed at one time, remote access availability, methods by which interlibrary loans or sharing of resources may be allowed (see Chapter 7 for additional information concerning licensing).
- Selection tools for electronic resources (see Chapter 3). This information should include whether selectors will only use selection tools or whether attempts will be made to identify reliable sources from Web searching.
- Selection criteria (see Chapter 3) that primarily affect electronic resources only (such as ease of use, searching capability, operating system platform and system hardware requirements, ease of downloading, and printing capabilities).
- Selection by the item or by collection of resources (such as a Web site containing lists of links) or both.
- Access issues (see Chapter 5), such as full MARC cataloging of Internet resources, or a "Webliography," or a list of links on the library's Web site, or some combination of these approaches. Depending on the level of effort needed to maintain the collection of available Internet resources, stability of those resources may be a problem, but they should not be ignored for that reason alone.
- Selection issues. When the same resources can be acquired in various formats and versions, which one will be selected? If an e-journal lacks advertisements, pictorial elements and the like, should it be considered as if it were exactly the same resource as the print journal? How is the librarian to decide whether the missing elements are important enough to warrant duplication of the item in the collection?
- Access versus ownership issues. Does the library prefer to own physical copies of resources regardless of form, when that is an option, or is access alone sufficient to meet the library's needs?
- Preservation issues (see Chapter 8 for additional information concerning preservation issues). Will the material be available for future users? This area includes issues of whether the library has the right to access a source over the long term (see Chapter 7) and whether the material will continue to be maintained in a format that will allow the user to access the material.
- Duplication/overlap issues between print and electronic re-

sources, and duplication of materials licensed in bundles from aggregators.
- Potential changes in the selection process (for example, committee versus individual selection) (see Chapter 3).
- Technical concerns in regard to staff and patron training, technical support, ease of installation, and technical compatibility with the library's existing hardware and software platform.
- For materials accessed remotely, availability and reliability of telecommunications, system servers, and the like.

The rapid nature of change associated with today's libraries calls for collection development policies that are more flexible than those that have typically been used in the past and that can encompass all the available formats of information resources, including both locally owned resources and resources that can be accessed remotely on the World Wide Web. An integrated collection development policy approach is, it must be concluded, the only approach to take.

INTERNET RESOURCES

With the emergence and tremendous growth of the World Wide Web, there are now a multitude of essentially free resources that can be accessed by any library's users. Every day, more government documents and scholarly publications are being made available on the Web, and sometimes they are exclusively available in the Web format. Thus, another important consideration for many libraries will be the question of ownership, as opposed to remote access only to electronically available publications. Remote access to Internet or Web-based resources certainly allows for much wider access, potentially for greater ease of use by the library patron, and perhaps for lower local maintenance costs for upgrading, storing, and troubleshooting than are typical for electronic resources purchased for local use.

When the library is selecting nonproprietary Internet resources, several additional factors will need to be taken into account and a number of special issues should be considered:

1. Selection and accessibility, as opposed to collecting/purchasing.
   The Internet is a "big place." What tools and how much time will selectors use to locate Internet resources to add to the library collection? It is all too easy to get engrossed with Web searching to the detriment of other duties.
2. Space and cost restrictions generally do not apply.
   Without such factors as space and cost to consider, new selec-

tion criteria must aid selectors in choosing one resource over a similar one of the same level of reliability and accuracy.

3. New types of materials can be "collected."

Items which may have once seemed too ephemeral or fragile for the library's collection may now be "collected" on the Web.

4. Access is to dynamic rather than static resources.

The content of a selected Web site changes from day to day. Consider the implications of having selected materials that may change radically over time and may suddenly include materials that your community might find objectionable.

5. Resources are more likely than the corresponding printed resources to be examined as a whole.

Web and Internet materials will probably be more thoroughly examined before selection than print materials presently are, simply because without examination "on screen" it is usually difficult to determine "ease of use" problems, etc.

6. Multiple user access.

Instead of having one copy of an item that only one user may access at a time, the web allows for multiple simultaneous uses of a resource.

7. Accessibility and stability of the resources.

Is the material selected on a site that is stable in terms of its Web address? Is it accessible without too many server problems or does it require extensive amounts of time to download?

All these issues need to be addressed in the library's collection development policy if it is to be successful.

ACCEPTABLE USE POLICIES

Acceptable use policies may constitute a needed appendix to a library's collection development policy if the library offers unlimited Internet access as part of the electronic resource collection. Public libraries may find it particularly important to include appropriate online behavior rules in order to help protect children and to avoid offending other users. Of course, library policy and patron education can highlight many practical suggestions in this regard, but it should be clear that the ultimate responsibility for enforcement remains with the patron, or in the case of children, with their parents or guardians. Another area that an acceptable use policy should address is that of copyright violation or other misuse of electronic resources (see Chapter 7 for more on copyright issues). A number of libraries have found it appro-

Figure 2–1: Resources and Examples to Assist in the Development of an Integrated or Separate Electronic Collection Development Policy

Comprehensive Sites

Arizona Department of Library, Archives and Public Records. "Collection Development Training for Arizona Public Libraries." *www.dlapr.lib.az.us/cdt/index.htm*

Acceptable Use Policies

American Library Association. "Guidelines and Consideration for Developing a Public Library Internet Use Policy." *www.ala.org/oif/internet.html*

Carnegie Library of Pittsburgh. "Internet Access Policies." *www.clpgh.org/clp/policy/*

State Library of North Carolina. "Guidelines for Developing an Internet Access Policy." *www.dcr.state.nc.us/hottopic/pubacc/pubacc*

Separate Policies

Berkeley Digital Library SunSITE. "Digital Library SunSITE Collection and Preservation Policy." *www.sunsite.berkeley.edu/Admin/collection.html*

University of Iowa Libraries. "Policy for Electronic Resources Management." *www.lib.uiowa.edu/collections/policy.html*

University of Wyoming Libraries. "Collection Development Policy on Internet Resources." *www-lib.uwyo.edu/cdo/cp_internet.htm*

Integrated Policies

Florida Atlantic University Libraries. "Collection Development Policy: FAU Libraries." *www.fau.edu/library/cd_fau.htm*

Morton Grove Public Library. "Collection Development and Materials Selection Policy." *www.webrary.org/inside/colldevintro.html*

priate to place their acceptable use policies on the Web. The American Library Association Web site contains the document "Guidelines and Considerations for Developing a Public Library Internet Use Policy" (*www.ala.org/alaorg/oif/internet.html*), which can be very helpful as a model when writing such a policy.

REVISION OF COLLECTION DEVELOPMENT POLICIES

Just like their traditional print collection counterparts, collection development policies that include electronic materials need to be revised regularly. Furthermore, since the world of electronic resources is changing so rapidly, with many new kinds of products and formats emerging almost daily, they now probably require revision more often, and require more attention or "tending to" than collection development policies with which libraries have typically operated in the past. Although a good collection development policy has always required careful attention to the problem of needed revisions, today's and tomorrow's information environment will make a dynamic collection development policy a necessity if the policy is to be of any real use to the library and its user community. Although the frequency and manner in which policies are revised will naturally be affected by the library's size and staff, a regular revision schedule that works well for the particular library's situation needs to be planned for and followed.

CONCLUSION

If a library has not already arrived at the happy stage in its development where there exist sufficient electronic resources available within its collection (whether physically owned or licensed for remote access or selected from free Internet resources), in all probability a new and integrated collection development policy will be needed in the near future. Electronic resources are becoming too pervasive to be relegated to "special" policies aimed at treating the new formats as something supplemental to the library's basic mission. Instead, electronic resource selection and management issues should be added to the library's current collection development policy so that emphasis can be placed on the needed or desired subject content rather than on the forms that content might take. All of the library's selectors, in every subject area of the collection or specialization of mission, will need to consider the addition of electronic resources in connection with other decisions made for the selection and acquisition of new books, serials, and audiovisual materials of all types. As with all collection development decisions, electronic resources require that a coherent rationale be established for the acquisition of each item. Then, once obtained, the electronic resource must be offered in an orderly manner with proper training for staff and users.

3 SELECTION: CRITERIA AND THE SELECTION PROCESS

Before beginning the selection process itself, it is imperative for the librarian to consider the needs of his or her library's user community. If librarians are to address successfully the many challenges presented and the opportunities that are now available through the provision and proliferation of electronic information sources, starting from a clear understanding of their library's basic missions and goals is a must. This is a basic necessity in order to establish the types and kinds of library resources and services that libraries should be offering to their users. As electronic resources are added to their collections, few libraries are likely to find themselves sufficiently prosperous to continue to maintain both their prior levels of acquisition of traditional print materials and the simultaneous acquisition of the newer, electronic forms of materials. The selection decisions a library must make therefore necessarily involve a form of intellectual triage. Deciding what items to cut and what items to keep is a process best grounded on a philosophical basis, determined by a thorough needs assessment analysis appropriate to the library involved, rather than on the ad hoc, item-by-item basis that is all too often utilized by many libraries.

Conducting a needs assessment need not be a daunting task. The traditional journalist's approach to writing a news column by determining **who, what, when, where,** and **how** constitutes an appropriate and easy-to-apply methodology for analyzing the measures on which to build a philosophically grounded collection needs assessment. Under this approach, you, as the librarian, need to consider:

- **Who**
  Who are the users of your library? Has your base of library users changed recently or is it likely to change as a result of adding electronic resources? If electronic resources and services are provided through the library's Web site, who is permitted to use these resources? For instance, may anyone with access to the library's Internet site use your electronic reference service or may only bona fide members of your institutional community do so (for example, are only the faculty and staff of a particular school or university permitted to have access)? The answers to these questions will go a considerable distance toward determining an appropriate selection approach for your library, because they affect both the quality and the quantity of the resources needed.

- **What**
  What materials or information does your library's typical user

usually need or ask for? What are the apparently unmet needs of your library's current and anticipated potential users? Digging a little deeper, what do they *really* want or need (as opposed to what they say they want or need)? Is there a demand for new services, and what new services do your users need? Can electronic access to resources (both in terms of staff and text) help to provide or facilitate the provision of such services? What level of computer expertise do your library's current and expected future users have? What is the potential usage level, that is, how many users do you anticipate will want access to the same resources at the same time or at the same location?

- **When**
  When will your library's users get the materials and information they want, or, more important, how long are your users willing to wait for resources? The spread of the electronic information environment has undoubtedly decreased the length of time most users are willing to wait for needed information. Simultaneously, the likely level of their ire when that length of time is exceeded has apparently risen geometrically. Access to electronic resources can, therefore, provide greater user satisfaction—since, for example, electronic resources usually don't circulate and are never at the bindery.

- **Where**
  Once specific materials are identified, from what locations do your library's users typically need to be able to access these materials? Do they prefer to use the resource only in the library or do they want or need remote access to the item? Do users want the library to deliver the documents electronically or are your users content for the electronic resource simply to direct them to a hard-copy source?

- **How**
  How can the library best obtain the information that is requested or needed? A mixture of qualitative and quantitative measures that brings in the views of a cross-section of potential users is a good approach to determining the answer to this question. The library could conduct focus group interviews with users and potential users to obtain information about user preferences, fears, and unmet needs in relation to information in general and electronic resources in particular. The library could also conduct a mailed or electronically delivered questionnaire or utilize telephone inquiries or face-to-face interviews with a random or purposefully selected sample of the library's current or potential

user community. These survey methods could then be supplemented with system statistics for those electronic resources your library already owns, as well as reference or interlibrary loan requests that have historically been required in order to acquire access to materials from outside the library so as to meet patron needs. Your integrated library system may allow you to gather data concerning the current use of electronic resources, the number of users of these resources, the number of searches they typically conduct and, more important, the number of successful searches, how electronic resources are usually accessed (in-house or remotely), the number of print commands issued, and a host of other report data that will assist you in the selection process.

It appears self-evident that local priorities and needs, as limited by any local constraints (such as the all-important constraints of limitations on funding) are essential factors that have to be considered whenever selecting electronic resources. However, sometimes in the rush to meet patron and administration demands to become more electronic (and hence more "modern"), the fact that a vendor shows up on your doorstep with an attractive short-term deal on a particular product that seems able to get the library out of a current jam can become an alluring alternative to a carefully considered program, and can thus often present a matter of paramount concern. Making decisions too hurriedly may staunch a wound, but a series of hasty decisions can and usually does lead to a feeling of utter chaos not only for the library's staff, but also for those library users who do not understand why the library's resources appear to lack coherence and consistency. It is thus extremely important for librarians with collection development responsibilities to monitor user needs and priorities while negotiating the tricky and rapidly changing terrain of electronic vendors and products.

SELECTION CRITERIA

In considering selection of an electronic resource, the following questions should always be asked:

1. Is the resource authoritative? Determining the accuracy of materials available through an electronic resource, and particularly those derived from Web resources, is critical to the selection and evaluation process. One of the strengths of the World Wide Web is the ease of publication and distribution of information to the

world; however, this strength is also its greatest weakness since it essentially places the burden on the information user to determine and evaluate the source of the Web site's information (that is, to do the very thing that collection development policies have traditionally attempted to do for libraries and their patrons over the years).

2. Does the technology make the content of the electronic resource accessible in a manner that better serves users' needs than does an existing equivalent print resource that the library already maintains or could acquire, perhaps at a lower cost? Some electronic products may actually be more difficult to use than their print counterparts, but others will offer significant improvements in the ways that a user can search for needed information.

3. Does the electronic resource fill current gaps in the print collection? Electronic products should not be acquired simply because they are there and available or "neat" and "cool," but rather they should add needed resources to the library's collection.

4. Does the electronic resource duplicate information or material that is already owned by the library? Due to the common practice of the bundling of electronic resources, libraries may sometimes find themselves forced to accept some duplication that would have never been contemplated or tolerated with print resources.

5. Will the library replace a current print resource with an electronic resource, and what are the pricing ramifications of doing so? Some electronic resources do cost less, but only if the library also takes the print version. Some publishers require the library to pay for the print version in order to be eligible to subscribe to the electronic one. On the other hand, some electronic resources really do cost less than their print equivalent, and in the case of those that are frequently supplemented, such as tax or legal services and reporters, the savings in filing labor costs can be enormous. Some electronic resources are priced so that there is an additional cost (above the price for the current version or issue) for access to the archives of the resources. In addition to price, one should also consider whether the electronic resource contains everything that is in the print version. Are all articles included in the electronic version, are advertisements deleted, are illustrations deleted, is the electronic product as well indexed as the print version? Is there an index at all or is there exclusive reliance on word searches, for example. And are any deletions in the electronic version important to your users?

6. If the electronic resource is licensed and not available for purchase (see Chapter 7 for more on licensing issues), can the library continue to meet its current obligations to local or state

consortia in regard to interlibrary loan or user access to materials if some materials are only available in restricted form?

7. Does the electronic resource require the purchase of additional computer hardware or software? Will it run on your current operating platform? For cost considerations, the selector may have to ensure that the format of an electronic resource is compatible with existing library hardware and software (unless there is equipment money available to support simultaneous purchases of hardware).

8. If an electronic product is selected, what format is the most appropriate to meet the library's needs? Would a CD-ROM product or an online product best meet the needs of the library and its users?

9. Does your library have enough computer resources to handle the additional user traffic that this product would likely generate? For small libraries, adding an electronic resource can be a significant problem; they simply may not have enough computers (or suitable space for computers) for patrons to access the new resource in a reasonable amount of time. This problem is particularly true if the library must cease carrying print versions in order to be able to purchase the electronic equivalent. A large set of print books, such as a multivolume encyclopedia, might be expected to be used by a number of patrons at the same time, but, if you only have one computer that can access a particular resource (or a number of electronic resources), only one person will be able to access the resource at a time.

The "Selection Criteria Worksheet for Electronic Resources" on page 30 will also be a useful tool for selectors.

SELECTION DIFFERENCES FOR INTERNET RESOURCES

Although most selection criteria typically used for determining the appropriateness of print resources apply equally in respect to Internet resources, a number of important distinctions need to be kept in mind:

- The librarian is truly only selecting materials, not collecting them. Internet resources selected are not likely to be housed on the library's computer other than temporarily; the resources are merely accessed from the library's catalog or Web site.

- The librarian may choose to select items that in print form were never considered for purchase. For example, the library may have acquired few pamphlets in print form due to problems in cataloging, shelving, and the difficulties in making the items available. The equivalent publication on the Web obviously does not present the same handling problems for the library.
- Cost, in terms of purchase price for the item, at least, is not likely to be a factor, but the librarian must consider the overall cost of maintaining links to the resource. A resource that is constantly moving and requires, therefore, constant URL maintenance and updating, either in the catalog or on the library's Web site, may well be so frustrating as to be deemed not worth the effort, even if the information it provides is of good quality.
- Selection of Internet resources tends to take place at a sort of macro level, while most print decisions tend to be made at the micro level, that is to say, Internet resources are typically chosen in a more generalized manner. Selecting Internet resources, therefore, can quickly lead to more duplication and result in the need for users to examine more unneeded or inappropriate resources in order to get to the ones they actually need. It is also important to remember that by selecting a Web site, you are in effect selecting everything that is linked from that page, and not all of those links will necessarily be needed by your library's user community.
- On the other hand, while print resources are much more likely than online materials to be chosen without actual examination of the item but rather through reviews or approval plans, Internet resources will typically be chosen generally only after personal examination by the selector. However, a number of the traditional selection tools are beginning to include reviews of Web sites, so the practice of choosing Internet resources may tend to become, over time, more similar to the methods traditionally used for selecting print resources.
- Some of the library's Internet resources may be actually created or published by the library itself, which is a circumstance that was not often the case with regard to traditional print resources.
- Access is a critical issue. If the server on which the resource resides is overtaxed and therefore slow to respond, or if it is often not available at all, the resource will probably not be selected by the library; likewise, technical reliability problems, no matter how accurate and authoritative the information provided by the site may be, can become a paramount concern if significant difficulties are encountered. An additional access issue to consider involves the number of users who may be provided with simultaneous access to a single item. A single-volume print docu-

ment may typically only be accessed by one user at a time, but the same resource, when made available on the Web, may usually be accessed effectively by numerous if not an unlimited number of simultaneous users.
- Archiving and preservation issues are obviously much more problematic with Internet resources than for traditional print materials. Quality Web sites come and go at the Web site owner's discretion (and sometimes whim), but a print resource, unless stolen, lost, or mutilated, will typically remain in the library's collection for a very considerable time.

SELECTION TOOLS

In order to make good selection decisions regarding electronic materials, you will first need to "corral" a group of titles with review information using both a local and global information perspective. Therefore, it is important to determine a set of resources to be used to gather titles and then to apply selection criteria to select among various materials having a similar subject-matter focus. The selector will be looking for tools that can help him or her answer the following types of questions:

- What is available? For an older title (and with electronic resources an "older" title may not be all that old) one must also add inquiries into its current availability. It existed once, and it was good, but is it still available?
- How much does it cost?
- Where can it be obtained?

A further consideration is quality, which must be judged both from a subject-matter and also a technical perspective:

- Does it deliver what is promised?
- Has it won any awards or been cited in bibliographies or reliable Webliographies?
- Is the vendor reliable? This assessment can be based on experience garnered through past purchases or upon recommendations of colleagues or reliable reviews.
- Is the resource authoritative? Electronic resources do not always benefit from the same formal filtering/vetting processes that have traditionally been in place with conventional print materials; and

thus, authority becomes a primary selection criteria that the selector may have to consider. The selection tools you choose that are best are those that help you determine the authority of the resource.

Internet and other electronic resources can be identified and evaluated through the use of reviews provided through both print and electronic resources. Perhaps a little ironically, printed guides to Internet resources abound, and, of course, many Web sites contain links to pages with evaluations, though the usually anonymous nature of these "reviews" can make them suspect. Many print review sources (such as *Library Journal, School Library Journal, American Libraries*, and *Choice*) also include reviews of electronic products and services. *College and Research Libraries News* has included Webliographies for particular subject areas for several years.

REVIEW SOURCES FOR WEB SITES AND OTHER ELECTRONIC RESOURCES

- **C&RL NewsNet: Internet Reviews** *www.bowdoin.edu/~samato/IRA/*
  This is an archive (updated monthly) of the abridged online version of *C&RL News*. It contains reviews of Internet resources, written by librarians.

- **Current Cites** *http://sunsite.berkeley.edu/CurrentCites/*
  Current Cities is an electronic newsletter that contains useful reviews of numerous electronic resources as well as print sources in various areas of information technology.

- **Educate Online** *www.educate.co.uk*
  Along with other resources, the Educate Online Web site contains a section titled "CD-ROM Reviews," which provides extensive reviews of CD-ROM products of all kinds. The reviews are arranged under broad subject area as well as a "newest" category. Although the Web site has a school orientation, other libraries should find the reviews useful as well. The Web site also contains reviews of new Internet Web sites and projects, and includes annotations plus a software review section.

- **Librarian's Index to the Internet** *www.sunsite.berkeley.edu/InternetIndex/*
  Librarian's Index to the Internet is arranged by subject, and tries to cover a wide range of areas. Each index entry contains the title of the Web resource, its Web address, and an evaluative

annotation. LIIWeek is a weekly announcement list containing those new entries that have been added to the Librarian' s Index to the Internet during the preceding calendar week. You can subscribe to LIIWeek by sending a message to listproc@ sunsite.berkeley.edu with the message "subscribe liiweek" and your name.

- **Library Journal Digital: WebWatch Archive** *www.ljdigital.com/ articles/multimedia/webwatch/webwatcharchive.asp*
  This is an archive of reviews of Web sites. Written by librarians, it can be a useful tool, but it contains a good bit of outdated material.

- **NewJour**
  NewJour, an electronic discussion list, can help you identify new electronic journals. To subscribe, send an e-mail message to listproc@ccat.sas.upenn.edu with the message "subscribe NewJour" and your name.

- **Publib Discussion List** *www.sunsite.berkeley.edu/Publib/*
  Publib Discussion List is an excellent source for information concerning resources available on the Internet, with a public library focus. Although this discussion list is certainly not entirely concerned with resource information, it is also still an excellent source for information about useful Web sites. Publib can be read from the Web site or from an electronic mailing list format. Instructions for subscribing to the electronic mailing list are provided on the Web site.

- **Scout Report** *www.scout.cs.wisc.edu/scout/report*
  Scout Report is a weekly electronic publication produced each Friday which provides reviews of valuable resources on the Web. Scout Report can be read from the Web site or from an electronic mailing list. Instructions for subscribing to the electronic mailing list are provided on the Web site.

- **TourBus** *www.tourbus.com*
  Twice a week, TourBus provides reviews on many informative and fun Web sites. TourBus can be read from the Web site or though an electronic mailing list. Instructions for subscribing to the electronic mailing list are provided on the Web site.

GENERAL REVIEW SOURCES ONLINE

The following are just a sampling of the sources that are available on the Web to help in selection. Although the focus of these Web sites is on print sources, some popular electronic products are reviewed.

- **Amazon.com** *www.amazon.com*
  Amazon.com provides access from its Web site to various lists of "opt" or "best" books, videos, CD-ROMs, and other materials. The selector also has access to peer reviews and standard review media. Some selectors find these peer reviews from readers to be helpful; they feel that the peer reviews may be more in touch with the materials that their users are likely to want or like.

- **Barnes and Noble** *www.bn.com*
  Barnes and Noble offers similar services to the material that Amazon.com offers, including peer reviews of materials.

- **BookWire** *www.bookwire.com*
  This Web site contains reviews and links to other review sources such as the Boston Book Review and Hungry Mind Review.

- **Borders** *www.borders.com*
  The Web site of this fast-growing book chain is noteworthy for its reviews and links to the New York Times Book Review.

OTHER SELECTION MEANS

In addition to being reviewed in more or less traditional ways, whether in print publications or on the Web, electronic resources often lend themselves well to other means of evaluation, including:

- Trial offers—Vendors of electronic resources may allow you to mount or link to their materials without cost for a trial period. After the trial period, one must either purchase or license the materials in order to continue using them. Trials are often advertised through e-mail and library Web sites. Thus more users are likely to try the products and offer advice to the selector than is likely to be the case for traditional print materials. Some libraries (and publishers) limit trial offers to staff use, but others open them up to their entire user population so that feedback from users, along with usage statistics, can be utilized in the final selection decision process. You will want to make sure that the trial conditions are equivalent to the actual use conditions that would apply if you purchased or licensed the product and that you do not receive a poor demonstration version.

- Demonstrations—Vendors will often be willing to come to your library and demonstrate their electronic products to you. Again, be sure that the conditions of the demonstration are as close as possible to what they would be if the product were purchased or licensed. For example, you don't want to see a demonstration of a Web product at 8:00 A.M. on Monday when Web traffic would probably be much lower than on, say, Wednesday at 3:00 P.M.
- Visits to other libraries—Another way to gauge the usefulness of a product is to visit a similar library that already has the product and to see it in action there. This approach also provides the opportunity to talk with that library's staff about the product and their experience with it. To be really useful, the library that is visited should have a similar technological setup and user base as yours.

SELECTION TEAMS

Instead of relying on individual selectors for the final selection decision, many libraries are today utilizing a team approach for the selection of electronic resources, an approach similar in some ways to the methods that many public libraries have traditionally used for the selection of audiovisual materials. Such teams will often include members from both public services and technical services departments. Bringing together a team with both subject and technical expertise can be a very effective method for selection of any material that is expensive and requires equipment and/or software for use. A carefully chosen team of three to five members can be constituted with persons of differing expertise and it can usually then manage subject-matter considerations and technical matters, and gather patron and staff input as appropriate. This team could also be responsible for producing documentation and training sessions after the electronic resources are acquired. In addition, establishing a planning and reviewing cycle with specified actions to occur at regular intervals, the team can go a long way toward helping to bring order to a potentially chaotic process. Because electronic products are still used in a rather unstable environment (that is, on the personal computer), embarking on an electronic acquisitions team approach requires team members to be open-minded and flexible. Change is constant and selectors must be able to make decisions in environments that are often more murky than crystal clear.

Figure 3–1: Selection Criteria Worksheet for Electronic Resources

Name of Product: _____

Publisher/Vendor: _____

Contact: _____

Phone/Fax/E-mail: _____

I.   Audience

    A.   Who will likely use the resource?

        [ ] General public   [ ] Researchers

        [ ] Students (K-12)   [ ] Library staff

        [ ] Students (College)   [ ] All of the above

    B.   Does this resource have broad appeal across all types of library users?

        [ ] Yes   [ ] No   [ ] Unknown

    C.   Will the resource require special training?

        [ ] Yes   [ ] No   If yes: [ ] Available at no cost from vendor

                                        [ ] Available for $_____

    D.   What type of user support is available?

        [ ] Unlimited support at no cost

        [ ] Unlimited support for _____ and then $_____

        [ ] Help Desk hours _____ Cost $_____

II.   Content

    A.   What type and breadth is the resource?

        [ ] Fulltext   [ ] Abstracts

        [ ] Bibliographic citations   [ ] Annotations

        [ ] Statistical   [ ] Graphics

        [ ] Other _____

Selection Criteria Worksheet for Electronic Resources (*Continued*)

    B.   What is the current size of the resource?

           Number of records/items/titles _____

           Megabytes _____   Number of CDs _____

    C.   What are the dates of coverage?

           [   ] Retrospective back to _____

           [   ] Current from _____ to _____

    D.   How will the information be updated?

           [   ] Daily   [   ] Weekly   [   ] Monthly

           [   ] Quarterly   [   ] Annually   [   ] Other _____

    E.   How unique is this resource to the library's current collection?

           [   ] New resource

           [   ] Equivalent of print resource already owned? Title? _____

           [   ] Equivalent of another electronic product? Title? _____

    F.   Is there a need for archival access?

           [   ] Yes   [   ] No   [   ] Unknown

    G.   Quality checks

           [   ] Reviews   [   ] Demonstrations in-house

           [   ] Free trial offer   [   ] Demonstrations in other library/vendor settings

III.   Costs

    A.   Initial costs for the resource?

           Setup/access cost $_____

           Storage cost $_____

           Maintenance cost $_____

Selection Criteria Worksheet for Electronic Resources (*Continued*)

    B.   Content/licensing costs?

        Flat rate/unlimited access $_____

        Flat rate for _____ simultaneous users $_____

        Flat rate per simultaneous user $_____

        Based on FTE users $_____

        Rate based on library holding of

        print resource $_____

        Other _____ $_____

IV.   Access

    A.   Where does the resource reside?

        [   ] Vendor's server   [   ] Library's server   [   ] Web

        [   ] Other_____

    B.   What are the hardware and software requirements? If the resource requires special software, does it reside on the vendor's server or on the library's server or on individual workstations?

    C.   What is required to access the resource?

        [   ] IP secured address   [   ] Password secured   [   ] Other_____

        [   ] Proxy server   [   ] Bar code

    D.   Statistical reports are available?

        [   ] Annually   [   ] Quarterly   [   ] Monthly   [   ] By request

        [   ] Individual subscriber basis   [   ] Consortium or group level only (if applicable)

    E.   If this product is later canceled, will the library still have access to the information that was once licensed?

        [   ] Yes   [   ] No

    F.   Does the library have permission to locally archive the resource?

        [   ] Yes   [   ] No

Selection Criteria Worksheet for Electronic Resources (*Continued*)

V.   Licensing Arrangements

    A.   Can you download a copy from the electronic version?

        [ ] Printed copy [ ] Electronic file copy

        [ ] Both   [ ] Neither

    B.   Do you have the ability to make a copy for interlibrary loan purposes?

        [ ] Yes   [ ] No

    C.   Are there restrictions on users?

        [ ] Local, in-building access only

        [ ] Remote access if authenticated

        [ ] Walk-ins to the library may use

        [ ] Must restrict to registered borrowers or faculty and staff or organization members

VI. Ease of Use and Appropriateness

How would you respond to the following statements about the product:

    A.   The search engine for this product is powerful.

        [ ] Strongly agree   [ ] Agree   [ ] Disagree   [ ] Strongly disagree

    B.   The number of access points available is sufficient for most users.

        [ ] Strongly agree   [ ] Agree   [ ] Disagree   [ ] Strongly disagree

    C.   Overall this product is easy to use.

        [ ] Strongly agree   [ ] Agree   [ ] Disagree   [ ] Strongly disagree

    D.   If there is a print equivalent, this product faithfully reproduces the print original.

        [ ] Strongly agree   [ ] Agree   [ ] Disagree   [ ] Strongly disagree

        [ ] Not applicable

    E.   This product has the potential to be heavily used by patrons.

        [ ] Strongly agree   [ ] Agree   [ ] Disagree   [ ] Strongly disagree

CONCLUSION

The selection of electronic resources continues to be a troubling proposition for many libraries. Selection in today's libraries covers the traditional factors plus a number of new technical and cost factors. The tendency of vendors to bundle or package a number of resources/titles/images has moved more of the selection process from a title-by title selection approach to an aggregate approach. This new approach includes new decisions as to tolerable amount of duplication, consideration of differences in search engines, and analysis of differences in ease of use of the product, and other such factors. Nevertheless the selection process remains important. Because of these various new technical issues, selection may best be accomplished through a team approach that incorporates members having both subject-matter and information technology expertise.

4 BUDGETING AND ACQUISITIONS

The work of a library's acquisitions staff is changing somewhat with the advent of electronic resources and the concomitant change in emphasis from direct ownership of materials to access to or licensing of those materials. Because many acquisitions functions are therefore moving from a purchasing to a licensing environment, selectors must take into account copyright and contract law considerations. Another important issue that arises is determining what part of the library's budget can be used to purchase the electronic resources. And, if the material is to be purchased at the document-by-document level, should the patron or the library bear the cost for the article or item? In cases of substitution, does (or should) it matter whether the library previously owned the resources, but canceled the resource subscription or discarded the item in order to rely exclusively on document delivery services for the item? Consideration and resolution of these questions is a central issue in the acquisitions process for virtually any library today.

THE ACQUISITIONS PROCESS

After the electronic product to be selected is initially identified, the standard acquisitions functions of verifying the bibliographic information of the product, identifying the pricing options applicable to it, and determining terms of its availability are matters that become equally challenging. A single database or electronic journal may be available from multiple sources, each with different search software, retrieval capabilities, and user functions. These choices, with their related purchase, lease, and subscription options, all naturally affect the price and availability of the product. To investigate these details, acquisitions librarians must work with vendors or distributors that specialize in electronic resources, or with their standard vendors who also offer electronic products in addition to their usual inventory. Of course, some electronic products may be purchased only directly from a particular publisher or distributor, as that particular company may not deal with aggregators.

Even placing the order for an electronic product may become something of a challenge, since the standard library ordering procedure may often need to be supplemented by a product-specific order form. In using such forms, often the library is asked to provide additional details about the anticipated use or number of users of the product, the equipment that will be used by the library, and the expected permanent location of the product. At this point, a license agreement may need to be signed before the purchase order will be accepted by the vendor. In the case of some vendors, the library may see the license agreement for a product only after the order is placed and the product has arrived; such a process may necessitate holding up the use of the product until the agreement can be negotiated and signed.

PRICING MODELS FOR ELECTRONIC RESOURCES

For materials accessed remotely, most, but not all, scholarly electronic publications produced today require a subscription or license in order for the library's users to access the product. The way the pricing works varies somewhat from product to product. A few of the more common models are the following:

- If the library subscribes to the print version of the resource, the electronic version can be accessed at no additional charge.
- If the library subscribes to the print version, there may be a small additional charge for access to the electronic version. Publishers following this model, however, often require subscription to the print product before they will sell the library an additional subscription to the electronic version.
- Some electronic versions are available without subscription to the print version, at the same subscription cost as the print product.
- Some publishers offer an electronic-only subscription for slightly less than the print resource.
- Some publications are only available electronically and they carry their own cost for subscription.
- Some publishers and aggregators operate on a "pure bundling" model where a library or consortium must license the entire list of their journals with no individual selections possible.
- Some aggregators of electronic journals and databases offer a pay-per-view option that allows users to enter an account already established or a credit card number to access articles from journals that are not on subscription.
- Many electronic products are, of course, freely available on the Web.

BUDGETING FOR ELECTRONIC RESOURCES

The information resources budget of most libraries has historically been known as the acquisitions or materials budget, with the materials traditionally purchased being, of course, principally print materials. As information typically provided by libraries expanded over the years to include nonprint materials, such as microforms and sound and video recordings, the cost of these materials was also included in the resources allocation schemes. In the 1980s, online searching costs began to be included in the typical library's information resources budget, and in the 1990s, leased information on CD-ROMs often became a part of that same budget.

Libraries generally do not receive additional or special-purpose funding for electronic resources, so that the costs of these resources are generally covered through the reallocation and redirection of existing money. Following selection decisions, funding issues regarding electronic resources are next in importance. Libraries generally take one or a combination of the approaches outlined below.

- All purchases of electronic products and subscriptions are taken from the general materials budget of the library.
- Some electronic products or subscriptions are taken "off the top" of the budget before the materials budget is allocated.
- Some libraries set aside a certain percentage of the materials budget for electronic resources, or they may set up a spending ratio of books to serials to electronic resources in order to make allocations.
- Some libraries allow a portion of their materials budget to cover hardware costs or processing costs as well as software costs.
- Some libraries require purchases of electronic products through team selection or at least with a check-off system so that a wide-ranging review of a product is made before it is finally selected for purchase. This approach is also helpful regarding the broad range of subject matters that may be included in an electronic product, so that coordination across disciplines and between subject specialists and technical experts can be achieved.

The model that a library chooses to utilize is very important, because a growing percentage of the budgets of all types of libraries is now being used for electronic resources, and this trend seems likely to continue and to become more evident in the near future.

CONSORTIUM PURCHASES

At one time in the not too distant past, library materials selection was generally an individual, that is to say, an item-by-item, process, with all the steps in the acquisitions process being clearly defined and usually pretty cut and dried. Most items were paid for individually, whether the item being acquired was a monograph, a serial, or an audiovisual selection. With electronic resources, there now exists a multitude of options for how materials may be acquired as well as a multitude of formats of the materials. The traditional primary skills of a selector (that is, subject knowledge and a knowledge of the publishing structure for the particular discipline involved) now must be augmented by knowledge of the technical aspects of the materials, consideration of the copyright and licensing issues that may be implicated, as well as familiarity with the various bundles of electronic materials (to compare coverage and prices). Ideally, selection must be conducted through a team approach and should ensure inclusion on the team of members possessing specialized knowledge in these various areas.

Since electronic resources are often much more expensive than print ones, many libraries are coming together for joint or group purchases of electronic products. Electronic products have really made joint purchases a serious proposition for many libraries. In the past, librarians have talked a great deal about joint purchases, but such plans were all too often stymied when the question of where the material was to be housed came up for discussion. Everyone naturally wanted purchases on their own shelves, not on someone else's. But for electronic resources, group arrangements can often result in a substantial savings for individual libraries while also adding a vital layer of coordination and expertise at a central level. Such an arrangement is, of course, particularly beneficial for smaller libraries that may not have the technical expertise in-house to do all the necessary technical evaluations prior to purchase. On the other hand, this type of arrangement does add a level of bureaucracy to the selection process (but, depending on the library's size and budget, the additional administrative "cost" may be very worthwhile).

If a library is involved in multiple consortial arrangements, buying electronic resources in several different packaging arrangements can and usually will lead to undesirable duplication of titles and items. For libraries that are part of large municipal or state systems, funding bodies may, of course, be dictating these kind of purchases through a centralized acquisition system or by requiring libraries to share resources maintained on centralized servers.

Library consortia with paid training staff can help members plan for, acquire, and learn how to use and access systems and electronic databases. This network support may often be crucial for public and other libraries that do not enjoy a centralized computing center on which they may rely. Consortia can also spread such costs over a number of member libraries and thereby effect substantial savings. And since operational and maintenance costs should always be considered in the selection process, savings in these areas are important factors to be considered in the overall acquisitions process.

INFORMATION AT THE ARTICLE LEVEL

If document delivery is perceived to be part of the acquisitions process, then an important question to be asked is "Who should control the requesting of articles from a document supplier?" Put another way, should document delivery be a mediated process with a librarian making the acquisition decision or should users be able to make direct requests from the supplier?

If the library already owns the document needed, then the library may find it appropriate to block or otherwise prevent the user from making an external request (that will cost the library more to obtain, for a second time) for the particular resource. If a document delivery service is used instead of an existing library resource, the service could also justifiably be viewed as a "luxury" service—for which the user should logically pay. Of course, the resource may not be readily available for a number of reasons (such as at the bindery or off the shelf), so in such situations should there not also be in place a procedure to handle service problems due to local conditions?

Recognizing this problem, some libraries use the blocking services of a document supplier to prevent users from requesting items already owned, but many other libraries feel, even when document delivery costs are borne by the library, that potential user frustration (particularly where there are branch libraries or multiple campuses) outweighs the additional acquisition costs. Other libraries, doubtless for financial reasons, feel that users must foot the bill for document delivery services. It seems, however, that the position that users should pay for delivery must become less and less defensible as more and more libraries increasingly rely on online document services.

Figure 4–1: Checklist and Budget Worksheet

How is access to an electronic resource best achieved?

  I. Can the entire resource be owned outright or purchased by the library at a reasonable cost?

      ☐ Yes ☐ No

                                     Estimated cost: $_____

      If yes, does the library presently have access to the hardware/software necessary for users to access the material?

      ☐ Yes ☐ No

      If no, how much will access cost?

                                     Estimated cost: $_____

  II. Must the resource be licensed rather than purchased?

      ☐ Yes ☐ No

      If yes, at what cost per year? (Please consult Chapter 7 for licensing issues and concerns.) $_____ / annually

  III. Would it be cost effective to purchase at the title or at the article level?

      ☐ Title ☐ Article

      For example, rather than purchasing or leasing an electronic serial, would a document delivery supplier be able to meet the demand for the material at a lower price than purchasing/leasing the entire serial?

      ☐ Yes ☐ No

      If so, what supplier is available? _____

                        Estimated cost of document delivery: $_____

  IV. Is the library a member of a consortium that makes group purchases?

      ☐ Yes ☐ No

Checklist and Budget Worksheet (*Continued*)

Name of consortium: _____

If yes, consult with consortium management as to electronic products
for which the consortium has made arrangements for group
purchases.

Cost to library: $_____

If no, bring the product to the attention of consortium members for
possible group purchases.

WEB TOOLS

A variety of information resources are available on the Web to assist the acquisitions functions. Some of these resources have information specifically about electronic resources and others function as electronic resources for acquisitions librarians.

BOOKSTORE NAMES AND ADDRESSES

- **Africa South of the Sahara: Bookdealers** *www-sul.stanford.edu/depts/ssrg/africa/afrbook.html*
  This online global directory contains an alphabetical list of bookstores with addresses. Telephone and fax numbers as well as e-mail addresses are also often provided.

BOOK AND OTHER MEDIA REVIEWS

- **Booklist** *www.ala.org/booklist/index.html*
  Electronic counterpart to the print magazine.

- **The BookWire Index: Review Sources** *www.bookwire.com/index/Review-Sources.html*
  Provides links to numerous review sources on the Web.

- **Boston Globe Online: Book Reviews** *www.globe.com/globe/living/bookreviews/*

- **The New York Times on the Web Book Reviews** *www.nytimes.com/* (requires registration)

LISTS OF AWARD-WINNING BOOKS

- **American Fiction Prizes** *www-stat.wharton.upenn.edu/~siler/litlists/amfict.html*
  Lists winners of the Pulitzer Prize for Literature, National Book Critics Circle Award, National Book Award, L. A. Times Book Award, Pen/Faulkner Award back to 1970.

- **The Children's Literature Web Guide** *www.acs.ucalgary.ca/~dkbrown/awards.html*
  Comprehensive guide to English-language children's book awards.

- **Agatha Winners and Nominees** *http://users.erols.com/malice/malice5.htm*
  Contains lists of winners and nominees for this mystery genre award from 1988 to the present.

BEST-SELLER LISTS

- **bn.com (Barnes and Noble***) www.bn.com*
  This site has The New York Times Bestseller Lists.

SERIAL BACK ISSUE DEALERS' CATALOGS

- Alfred Jaeger, Inc. *www.ajaeger.com/*
  The Web site offers a limited number of this publisher's extensive inventory of over 40,000 titles. You can also e-mail requests for items not found through the Web database.

STOCK AVAILABILITY AND PRICES

- BookFinder.Com *www.bookfinder.com*
  Special search engine that allows you to check availability and prices for new and used books at a variety of bookstores and booksellers. It returns a list of titles that match your search and provides you with the opportunity to order directly from the bookseller.

CURRENCY EXCHANGE RATES

- Universal Currency Converter *www.xe.net/ucc/*

PUBLISHERS' ELECTRONIC MAIL ADDRESSES

- **International Directory of Email Addresses of Publishers, Vendors and Related Professional Associations, Organizations and Services** *www.library.vanderbilt.edu/law/acqs/email-ad.html*

PUBLISHERS' CATALOGS AND GENERAL INFORMATION

- **Publishers' Catalogues Home Page** *www.lights.com/publisher/*
  Catalog directory can be searched geographically (city, state, country) by subject, and alphabetically by publisher.

- **Directory of Publishers and Vendors** *www.library.vanderbilt.law.acqs/pubr.html*
  Alphabetical, geographic, and subject directory to various publishers' Web sites.

POSTAL INFORMATION

- **United States Postal Service** *www.usps.gov/*
  This site contains information about postage rates and fees, including international rates.

TELEPHONE INFORMATION

- **AmeriCom Area Decoder** *http://decoder.americom.com/*
  This Web site allows you to find the city if you have the area code or vice versa.

- **Telephone Directories on the Web** *www.teldir.com/eng/*

AGGREGATOR SERVICES

The following is a list of subscription agents that serve as aggregators of electronic journals and databases. This list is intended to be a representative, rather than exhaustive, compilation, and because of the quick-changing nature of the electronic publication business, the list is necessarily subject to alteration at any moment. More information about the services listed below can be obtained by contacting the company directly or through visiting their Web sites. Web addresses are provided below.

- *Blackwell's* **Electronic Journal Navigator** *www.blackwells.com*
  This service provides, to name just a few of its many useful features, keyword searching of article titles and authors, searching and browsing by journal title, and retrieval of articles by citation. It also provides immediate electronic delivery of articles to the user's desktop.

- **EBSCO Online** *www.ebsco.com*
  This service offers searching by keyword and by Boolean operators as well as by publication year or range of years, and by volume or issue number. Natural-language searching is also al-

lowed. A "shopping cart" option facilitates online ordering. "Journal Details" pages provide additional publisher information, including descriptions of the editors, editorial guidelines for manuscript submissions, and other related Web resources.

- **Information Quest (IQ)** *www.eiq.com*
  This service allows concept searching based on words with similar meanings. Retrieval goes beyond truncation, by taking into account those words that are similar in meaning regardless of spelling. The service also provides for query-by-example or "more documents like this." Individual articles can be purchased for fax delivery, with added fees for copyright permission, delivery, and fax surcharge (if applicable). Current awareness services for tables of contents and articles can also be set up for individual users.

- **SwetsNet** *www.swetsnet.com*
  Provides a single catalog of all the serials titles in the SwetsNet service, plus tables of contents and abstracts. Full text can usually be delivered in Adobe PDF format. Direct links from a library's Web-based catalog (or from the Web) and full-text searching of the library's own subscriptions are also supported.

CONCLUSION

The process of budgeting for and acquiring electronic resources present new challenges for acquisition librarians. The entire concept of an information resources budget often becomes murky regarding what can and cannot be paid from it. We as librarians have always worked on the principle that items paid for from the resource budget were owned and permanently retained by the library. Now we may be acquiring resources for a particular patron through document delivery; the document never "sees" the library shelves. The information resources budget may or may not include necessary equipment purchases for using the resource. In addition, the new ways we can purchase or lease materials also bring challenges for the acquisitions librarian. Many of the new Web resources make many of the routine aspects of acquisitions work easier, but they do add another layer to the already complicated nature of materials acquisition.

5 ORGANIZATION AND ACCESS TO ELECTRONIC RESOURCES

Undoubtedly, libraries today expend the greatest proportion of their management efforts and resources in providing access to the new electronic forms of information resources, and particularly networked electronic information. This trend is partially because of the sea change in library holdings that has occurred in recent years due to the proliferation of those resources. It is also likely because the universe of electronic resources is generally not as well managed as that of traditional print resources.

As with any print resource, once an electronic information resource is selected, the library needs to provide an organized methodology for making its users aware of the resource and for ensuring that they can and know how to access it. Traditionally, libraries have been concerned with the proper handling, storage, and presentation of physical volumes or items and tracking them through the various procedures that preceded their availability on the library's shelves. We, as librarians, either cataloged such items (books and audiovisuals) or created serials lists (as a replacement for or as an addition to cataloging) with holdings for serial titles. Initially, electronic resources were treated differently by libraries. It was assumed that patrons knew that there existed somewhere in the library a publicly accessible computer station and that a CD-ROM or other similar product was available for use at that computer station or, it was further assumed, everyone "knew" to consult the reference librarian in order to conduct an online database search.

Nowadays, of course, electronic products have proliferated to the extent that not even the librarians can have much hope of keeping up with all that is currently available, and some type of formalized organizational structure for these products is therefore needed. Unlike in the traditional print environment, the organization of Web-based resources also brings with it the tasks of maintaining and updating the links to those resources. Even with the application of selection criteria that emphasize the relative stability of the resource proposed for inclusion within the library's available resources, URLs will still change.

Users today are far more likely to be suffering from an overload of information than from a lack of information. Bringing structure and form to electronically available information requires an examination of several basic questions:

- How do we know when an electronic issue of a journal has been acquired and "checked in"?
- Is the resource available only on certain machines in the library, or is the resource available to remote users through a Web catalog or library Web site?
- Should a library catalog all the titles contained in a large package licensed from an aggregator?
- How do we keep track of the changing titles and contents of databases to which a library may subscribe through a vendor or aggregator?
- Should the catalog point to individual titles or only to a particular vendor's Web site?
- How do we guide users to the best sources of electronic resources, as opposed to providing a search engine that retrieves, for example, 1,000 hits?
- If electronic resources are made available to remote users, how does the library authenticate those users in order to stay within the terms of the licensing agreements for the materials?

These questions all present very real challenges for today's librarians, and the methods of addressing these challenges are considered in this chapter.

LEVELS OF ORGANIZATION OF ELECTRONIC AND WEB RESOURCES

The first thing to consider is how organized you are presently. Libraries pass through phases or levels of organization in implementing access to and organizing their electronic products, passing all the way from an initial no-formal-organization-at-all stage to the full MARC cataloging of the items. These phases can be categorized as five levels of organization.

- **Level 1: No organization**
  At Level 1, the library simply offers users open Web access and is in effect operating as a sort of information utility. No formalized guidance is provided regarding the value of the resources, and electronic products available on the library's public computers are not cataloged. If there is any advantage to a Level 1 organization, it is purely in terms of short-term cost. Doing nothing usually appears to be the easiest approach, and, in all fair-

ness, tends to reflect not so much an inherent laziness in the librarians as a sort of "deer in the headlights" bewilderment—things change so fast in the electronic environment that just keeping the access available is seen as good enough. On the other hand, it indubitably appears that the Level 1 library adds no value for the user and may see itself becoming increasingly irrelevant.

- **Level 2: Selective lists or Webliographies**
  Here the library compiles either a list, or annotates a list, of what it judges to be reputable Web sources. These lists are hyperlinked on a computer page to provide a method of taking the user directly to the recommended Web sites. Many smaller libraries are now using this approach to point to other libraries' lists of selected resources. Linking appropriate Web resources to a library's Web site is a standard way to provide users with points of reference and a gateway for locating librarian-selected information on the Web. Level 2 libraries may also provide lists of locally owned CD-ROM products and/or designate workstations for different products, but at Level 2, such resources are still not cataloged. Level 2 constitutes a major step up from Level 1, and it enjoys the significant advantage that the costs of implementation are not too great, though careful work and constant maintenance is needed to avoid such pitfalls as a hodgepodge of dead links.

- **Level 3: Addition of metadata**
  At Level 3, the Level 2 lists are supplemented through the addition of metadata to selected Web resources that are housed on a local server to facilitate retrieval. These resources may be searched from the library Web site, from the electronic catalog, or through both methods.

- **Level 4: Mixed model**
  Libraries at Level 4 catalog the physical items purchased, but remotely accessed resources are linked through a library Web site, as in Level 3. Librarians using the mixed model generally feel that, once they have developed Web-based subject pages, it is usually redundant also to include these resources in the library's general catalog. At first glance, this method seems inconsistent, but librarians are most likely concerned, and rightly so, with the volatility of Web addresses and content and the level of staffing needed to keep the developed pages current. Thus, many libraries are following this model as a simple expedient due to a shortage of staff and staff expertise to perform full MARC cata-

loging for all their electronic resources. This model can be advantageous, obviously, but having to look in multiple places for materials will cause many patrons to use one or the other resource and either be unaware of or unwilling to search in the other location.

- **Level 5: Full MARC cataloging of electronic/Web resources**
  Those libraries at Level 5 will use one of three approaches:

  - Catalog all those electronic resources that are either owned by the library or maintained on its local system. Since these resources are under the control of the library, many of the objections to cataloging such resources are negated since neither the resource address nor the content will change without the library being aware of the update. If the resource is taken down and made unavailable, it will be the library's decision, and not that of an outside agency over which the library has no authority.
  - Catalog those significant resources that are anticipated to be heavily used by local patrons and/or library staff. Although not all of these resources will be under the control of the library, the selected nature of the items, coupled with the presumed relative stability of these major resources, makes their bibliographical control neither too difficult nor too time consuming.
  - Catalog all items identified by subject specialists or collection development librarians that fit the collection development policy of the library. This last option, which is arguably the ideal, requires a substantial commitment of time both from a collection development and a cataloging perspective. All the problems with Web instability, constant changing of electronic titles included in bundles from aggregators of electronic serials and databases, and changing coverage in the databases and electronic serials, are also implicated, meaning that considerable maintenance on an almost daily basis is required.

The use of computer networks to deliver information has resulted in a proliferation of available electronic resources—journals, government publications, statistics, and other research materials. It is natural that librarians, and particularly catalogers, have taken an active role in organizing and providing pathways to this kind of information. For many libraries there is a more or less logical progression through these options and through the levels of organization described above. As more and more electronic materials are considered to be part of the library's collection, more and more work is required to organize and make these materials accessible to the library's clients.

Although the World Wide Web has its own directory structures and searching tools, these provide neither the precision of a controlled vocabulary nor the variety of searching capabilities that are generally available through a MARC cataloging record typically provided in an online catalog, and particularly a Web-based online catalog. Full cataloging is thus an ideal that must be considered a worthy goal, even if it might not ever be fully achievable in the electronic information environment.

AUTHENTICATION OF USERS

Authentication of users constitutes an important aspect of any electronic information delivery system and presents a plethora of questions, such as:

- Who has access to your electronic resources?
- Do you have a well-defined set of clients or do you serve the general public?
- Once you have defined your clientele, can your users use electronic resources from their home or office or must they come into the library?
- Do you have branches or remote locations where users will want to access these products?
- If you have cooperative agreements with other libraries or organizations, can their users access your electronic resources?

All of these questions play a part in decisions about what authentication method is best for your particular library and its clients.

Using electronic resources increasingly involves controlling access to licensed databases or resources. Controlled access involves a two-step process. First there must be some method of identifying who the user is, often referred to as "authentication." Second there must be a method of ensuring that the authenticated user is in fact allowed access to the resource, often referred to as "authorization." (Note: More techniques are now available for user authentication than will be discussed here, including everything from the sorts of biometric identification techniques that once seemed the exclusive province of James Bond movies, to the more mundane—but still sophisticated—"smart" cards and so forth. But it should be noted that these techniques tend to work best and make the most sense in smaller organizations. The intent here is to discuss various common methods that libraries not contained within specialized organizations, or that do not serve a very specialized group of users, are using to authenticate and authorize their patrons successfully.)

As far as users are concerned, subscription or access validation, including both the authentication and authorization steps, should occur in the background so that it is transparent to the user if possible. The ideal situation would be for the library to provide access to all its electronic resources for all users regardless of where they are physically located. Once users are authenticated they should be able to use all resources—the authentication process should occur only once, rather than separately for each resource. Librarians should seek licensing contracts for electronic resources that allow for flexibility in the authentication or validation of their users.

Publishers have set up and developed a number of standardized ways of allowing remote access to their resources. These methods include:

- Passwords or credential-based approaches—Most librarians do and should not want to subscribe to products that require users to enter passwords in order to use the resource. Passwords are generally a burden for librarians—because usually the library must maintain a database of valid users and passwords and then provide users with those passwords, as well as deal with the problems of forgotten passwords and the revoking of passwords when the user is no longer a registered or authorized user. In most instances of resources maintained for public use, passwords are a real (and usually unjustifiable) headache for the library staff.

    A variation on password authentication could include the use of student identification numbers or codes that are assigned by the academic organization or, in the case of public libraries, barcodes added to the library cards of clients. This approach then allows authorized users to use numbers or codes that are standardized for a particular organization, as opposed to passwords separately assigned by the vendor. The vendor then can recognize at least a consistent pattern, if the actual numbers or codes are not provided, that indicates authorized users. This approach can be especially effective when resources are licensed for use by a consortium.

- IP source addressing approaches—Database and electronic journal vendors usually allow IP authentication for a specific range of IP addresses. Since this approach requires no special software and little support from library staff, this form of authentication is relatively simple for single-building and possibly campus usage (unless the campus is large, with several IP domains where configurations can quickly become complex and/or are frequently changing). It should be noted that IP address detection does cause problems for remote users. For users outside this range of IP

Figure 5–1: Proxy Servers

Proxy-based approaches still must employ an internal authentication and authorization system to control use of the proxy server. The library therefore must maintain an internal database of user names and passwords. Proxy server software runs on a Web server and is generally available at no additional cost for most server platforms. Simple in concept, the software provides a single point where user names and passwords are checked against a database of valid users; if the information provided is correct, the client is logged onto the proxy server. Any subsequent access requests come from the IP address of the proxy server and not the individual client's IP address, thereby making resources that require IP address authentication available to a remote user.

There are three main types of proxy: manual or mechanical, automatic, and reverse proxy. A **manual or mechanical proxy** requires the user to edit his or her browser settings, and once these settings are changed, the browser routes all of the client's Web requests through the library's proxy server, not just the requests that require a proxy. After the changes in the browser settings are made, the operation of the proxy becomes transparent to the end user. An **automatic proxy** eliminates the extra network traffic through the proxy server by allowing the client's browser to control which requests are actually sent to the proxy server. A **reverse proxy** is generally used as an additional means of security as it resides outside a firewall, sending and receiving client requests through the firewall to the specified server. The reverse proxy server rewrites the URL returned to the user so that it appears to come from the reverse proxy server instead of the actual host. The use of a reverse proxy is thus also completely transparent to the user, but its disadvantage is that it will not work with any resource that requires absolute, as opposed to relative, URLs.

Some authors use the term "application-level" proxy for proxy servers that forward requests where appropriate, but do not rely on protocol mechanisms (not limited to Web operations but could work with telnet applications, for example) as does the manual or mechanical proxy.

addresses, another layer of software, called proxy server software (see page 53), must be provided by the library. IP authentication is generally the method favored by most libraries. Libraries have generally overcome the problems with this approach by setting up proxy servers so that once users connect to the server and establish proxy server access, they appear to the remote server as coming from an authorized account.

- User account coupled with IP source detection—In this case, the user provides information about his or her right to have access to the resource, such as institutional affiliation or a subscription number from an institutional subscription. The user then creates an ID and password for future use. The vendor then may base access solely on the ID and password or may also use IP detection. Another approach is called an X.509 certificate, which gives a particular machine the right to the use of a particular name. The name is verified by checking with a "certificate authority." The certificate carries an expiration date which can be revoked. A revocation list can be maintained by the organization, and this list will be computer-checked before a user is allowed to access a resource. In addition, hybrid systems are becoming available that combine aspects of proxies and certificates.

These issues of authentication are multiplied when libraries jointly purchase or license electronic resources through a consortium or other resource-sharing collaboration. In such group licensing situations, verifying that a requester is indeed a valid member of a specified user community is potentially even more difficult. A central identity or proxy system is probably not usually feasible, so the group license agreement must be carefully constructed to allow for an authentication method that will work for each member of the group. Vendors may allow different means of authentication for different members of the group as appropriate to the particular situation.

Which choice is best for your library will necessarily depend a great deal on local factors. If you are a small special library with a fairly consistent client base, passwords may actually work well for you. If you are a large university library with students constantly being admitted and dropping out and with a large number of staff and faculty, the process of giving out and deleting passwords, providing lost password information, and password protection can create a nightmare. A library with a large and changing client base will no doubt prefer IP authentication with some kind of proxy server setup to allow remote users to access electronic resources.

It is also very common for different approaches to be utilized within the same organization based on classes of users or location of users.

For example, users at workstations in the library might be authenticated by IP address, but remote users might be authenticated in a different manner. Some systems can be configured so that an IP address check is done first and only if this check fails must the user provide a valid password or a valid user name and password. This approach provides a decent compromise.

CONCLUSION

In the very recent past, collection development librarians never needed to ponder organization and access issues when selecting resources for their libraries. Unfortunately, this is no longer the case. Since there often exists more than one source for an electronic journal or database or other resource, implications for organization and access are often extremely important issues for the selector. Access management must be addressed at a very practical level so that, from a user's perspective, the system facilitates and does not inhibit access to the electronic resources owned or licensed by the library.

From the library's standpoint, decisions made about the various ways to manage the organization of and access to electronic resources should not place an undue burden on library staff for its operation on an ongoing basis. But the library and vendor need to be assured that a hacker cannot "forge" a valid identity easily. In short, authentication and access management have emerged as major issues for libraries as they offer more and more electronic, networked resources.

6 EVALUATION AND ASSESSMENT

Collection assessment can be defined as the systematic, organized process of describing the state of a library's resources and their effectiveness at a particular time. Assessment requires that the collection be measured, analyzed, and judged according to specific criteria for relevancy, size, quality, and use. Librarians have generally thought of library assessments in terms of their library's book or serials collections, but assessment and evaluation are equally important for electronic resources and in determining the effectiveness of a library's mix of electronic and printed resources.

In the context of this handbook, the focus is on assessment of the electronic resources held or accessed through a particular library and how these materials assist the library in developing a collection that adequately meets the needs of its users. If a library has an integrated collection development policy, and in most cases it should, then the assessment must not be conducted of the electronic resources in isolation but rather in terms of how those resources fit into the library's overall collection.

If your library is operating under a separate collection development policy for electronic resources, an assessment can be configured solely to evaluate electronic resources. However, as stated in Chapter 2, the increasing array of electronic resources means that segregating them in policy/philosophy is probably detrimental to the overall planning and developing of the library collection as a whole.

ASSESSMENT DATA

In addition to statistics generally kept in libraries concerning the print collection's size and growth, libraries evaluating electronic collections will also need to collect data in the following areas:

- Type of Internet connection used by the library itself and that used by patrons to access the library remotely.
- Capabilities and distribution of computer workstations and printers provided in the library building.
- Internet and other network service costs, including the costs associated with remote dial-in capabilities.
- Web page and databases hits, searches, printing and the like.

ASSESSMENT ACTIVITIES

Collection assessment and evaluation covers a number of different activities. First, the proper assessment of a collection involves a comprehensive description of the library's resources at a particular point in time. This description will include not only an assessment of past collecting strengths and current collecting strengths, but also an assessment of what the library's future collecting strengths should be. An assessment project also evaluates the effectiveness of the library's collection in supporting the mission and goals of the organization of which it forms a part; it should lead to a plan of action detailing how the library's collection development activities should proceed in order to obtain the best match between the collection and the mission and goals of the library.

STANDARD AREAS OF DATA COLLECTION

Traditionally libraries have gathered qualitative and quantitative data in the following areas:

- Circulation statistics
- Title count
- Median age of item
- Shelf observation by subject experts
- Holdings checked against standard lists/bibliographies
- Interlibrary loan requests
- User surveys
- Focus groups

The ensuing information gained from these methods are equally important in terms of electronic resources and how they fit into the library's overall collection. However, there are some additional data collection methods, set out below, that can be used to obtain, relatively easily, the additional information that is needed concerning the library's electronic resources.

TECHNOLOGICAL ADDITIONS TO STANDARD DATA SOURCES

- Scripted user surveys/assessments—Provides users of electronic resources with a pop-up (or some other method) box on-screen, allowing them to rate the value of the resource to their information need (a user survey, so to speak, at the point of actual use of an electronic resource).
- Transaction log or Web log analysis—Provides data for analysis of user transaction activity at a Web site or in interaction with any electronic resource made available by the library. Some electronic resource vendors provide useful statistics about usage on a regular basis. These statistics can be used to make decisions concerning database renewal or the necessary number of simultaneous users. Examples of statistical data that might be gathered include number of queries per specific database, number of sessions, number of menu selections, number of items to examine, citations displayed, and the number of times users were denied access because the maximum number of simultaneous users was exceeded. Statistics, unfortunately, do not usually provide much information about the relative usefulness of a resource and whether the patron received exactly the information that was desired, but they can provide some information about how the particular product is being used; that information can then be supplemented through one or more of the qualitative assessment techniques.
- Network usage analysis—Measures the use of Web-based services by collecting network or terminal use statistics, such as the load on the network server or router, user access points, and number of users. This information shows network load and capacity and indicates what services are being used and how frequently.

QUALITATIVE TECHNIQUES

- Content analysis—Analyzes the content of a networked resource, including accuracy of information presented, aesthetics, readability, currency, and relevancy judgments. Although content analysis could also be performed on a print collection, this technique is much more likely to be used as a library collection assessment technique for electronic resources than for print resources. This technique is attractive because of the greater problems of authoritativeness that electronic resources typically present. Usability is also important to consider. Does the system "crash" when too many persons attempt to access it? Are the Web sites stable or do they move to other URLs frequently? Can you get "stuck" in the site with no clear way for the user to break out of it? Developing the answers to all of these questions requires devotion of significant time by librarians.

- Focus groups—Small groups of users are selected to explore key issues in such areas as electronic content, performance, and services. One might consider focusing on both heavy users of electronic resources and also reluctant users to get a full picture of user concerns and needs. Do users find the library's electronic resources to be user-friendly? Can they easily find their way around Web-based resource sites? Do they find the instruction and help provided on online sites to be adequate?
- Case studies—Particular "communities" of users, such as elementary school students, business-oriented users, researchers, etc., are selected in order to study in-depth their use of your electronic resources and how electronic resources contribute to their needs and particular uses.

The above quantitative and qualitative measures can be used to describe essential characteristics about the library's collection, such as:

- Collection adequacy to support library services—Can the materials owned or accessed from the library supply the information needs of the appropriate percentage of library users? Each library must decide for itself, based on available staff and resources, what percentage makes sense for its particular situation.
- Formats and types of materials acquired—What kinds of materials are being acquired and, second, what kinds of materials should be acquired in order to meet the demands of local patrons?
- Usage patterns—Both in-house use and circulation should be considered. Do multiple patrons need simultaneous access? Do users need access from home or office?
- Language of materials acquired compared to circulation and ILL requests. Does the library need to provide popular and/or scholarly materials in Spanish, Chinese or other languages?
- Reading levels acquired compared to items circulated—Does the reading level of materials acquired match the reading levels of the library's users.
- Current priorities compared to current usage and requests—For example, do the current priorities for materials as reflected in

your budget match current patterns of usage as reflected in circulation statistics or in requests made to librarians and staff at circulation or reference desks? Does an analysis of interlibrary loan requests reveal an area of current demand, but few materials to support that demand are being acquired by the library?

Collection maintenance actions determined from collection assessments include:

- Addition decisions—In examining the data collected, which titles or groups of materials does the library need to acquire?
- Preservation and conservation decisions—Did data collection identify materials of local or heavy use that require preservation action?
- Replacement decisions—What lost or mutilated or heavily worn materials are still in demand by patrons?
- Updating decisions—Where has your collection become outdated and in need of replenishment with newer materials?
- Weeding decisions—Are there areas in the collection that are no longer being used? What materials have become too outdated to be of use to clients?

Some internal library factors play an important role in either the location of resources by patrons or in how the library operates. They need to be considered when planning an assessment project because they can affect both the data collection process and the interpretation of those data. These factors include:

- Cataloging and indexing of resources—Are the resources being evaluated, properly cataloged, and indexed so that clients can find the resources? Buying an electronic resource and not providing proper access mechanisms dooms it to underuse no matter how outstanding its quality.
- Screen display—Is it clear and are its instructions easily understood? Does it load quickly on the computer?
- Is the software flexible enough to accommodate users with disabilities?
- Is reading level separation adequate? This factor can be crucial, particularly in a public library setting.
- Circulation or use counting procedures—Is the library accurately accounting for use? Are both in-house and remote use being adequately measured?
- Collection management policy selection criteria—Has the library established adequate selection criteria and are those criteria being followed?

- Purchasing and weeding data record-keeping procedures—Are proper procedures in place to evaluate a product correctly?
- Collection subunits—Particularly in public libraries, the way resources are distributed among various subunits of the collection can be vital for the effective use of the resource. For example: Should it be available from the children's room? Near the popular fiction collection?

TIPS ON MANAGING AN EVALUATION PROJECT

The preceding pages have outlined a number of data items that could be collected in a number of ways. Obviously, no one assessment or evaluation project will use all of them, so it is necessary to consider first what you really want or need to learn as a result of an evaluation project. First you must have firm goals in mind for the project, know what audience or audiences it is intended for, and then determine what data are needed for the purpose/goals that you have stated. Simply collecting data for the purpose of collecting data will not result in useful information about your electronic resources. You may collect so many data that it is impossible to see the forest for the individual trees. So before you engage in data collection, carefully determine what data are really required.

Once you have determined what data are needed, then consider how you will select the data. Data that can be objectively obtained from the report module of your online system, or from translation log analyses, will be more accurate than if you depend on users' perceptions of what they did. Such data are often easier to obtain and tabulate as well. However, a mix of qualitative and quantitative measures will give you a better feeling for the overall picture of your electronic resources and how they are accepted and used by patrons. Researchers generally agree that the use of more than one method gives a much more accurate picture of the "true" situation. Again, before collecting the data, think about how you will analyze the data. This step is very important in the planning stages since you don't want to get to the end of the data collection phase and discover that you failed to collect a vital piece of data that you really need when you begin your analysis.

Now you are ready to collect your data. Be sure that everyone involved in data collection knows exactly what to collect and be sure that they do so consistently. Instructions and training of data collectors is critical to the success of any evaluation project. Once the data are collected, turn them over to the person/group who will actually conduct the data analysis. Then, when the objective portion of the analysis is complete, remember that interpretation is key. For example, is a particular electronic resource not being used because its content is not needed (a collection development problem), patrons do not know it exists (a marketing problem), patrons do not understand how to use it (a training problem), or patrons cannot obtain access to a workstation to use the product (a hardware availability problem)? This is an area where the use of one or more of the qualitative measures will help you make the correct interpretation. Users are the best persons to tell you why they are not using a resource, but the analysis of usage statistics will never give you that slant on the issue.

Last but not least, always write up your findings. In fact, you may wish to write more than one report based on the intended audience. In-house, you may want more detailed information to help staff make selection and policy decisions. Externally, by contrast, you may want to prepare a more general report that provides an overall view for board members, faculty, and patrons. Also, keep in mind that different constituencies may be interested in different data as they may have significantly different perspectives about library resources.

CONCLUSION

Remember that the evaluation of electronic resources is a new and growing area of interest in the library and information science field. While in the past we have attempted from time to time to evaluate various online services, the increasing array of electronic resources in libraries today is causing increased interest, but as yet there are no ineffably "tried and true" methods. It was inevitable that we would start out using data collection methods originally intended for print materials, and then gradually add more and more data to be collected that is strictly for electronic resources. This change will lead to more methodologies for data collection that are specifically geared toward electronic resources. We are learning more and more about doing such assessments all the time, so stay tuned!

Figure 6–1: Work Form for an Electronic Resources Evaluation Project

I. What are our three main goals (external and internal) of the project?

  1. _____

  2. _____

  3. _____

II. Why are we conducting the project, i.e., who is our intended audience?

  1. _____

  2. _____

  3. _____

II.a. Who will conduct the project?

  ☐ Library Staff   ☐ Consultant   ☐ Library Staff with aid of a Consultant

III. Which method or methods of evaluation will be used?

  1. _____

  2. _____

  3. _____

  4. _____

IV. For each method, what data will be collected?

  Method 1: Data to be Collected

  1. _____

  2. _____

  3. _____

  4. _____

Work Form for an Electronic Resources Evaluation Project (*Continued*)

Method 2: Data to be Collected

1. _____

2. _____

3. _____

4. _____

Method 3: Data to be Collected

1. _____

2. _____

3. _____

4. _____

V. Will the library staff need training in data collection? ☐ Yes ☐ No

If so, how and by whom will the training be provided?

1. _____

2. _____

Estimated Cost: $_____

VI. How will the data be analyzed?

Data from Method 1: _____

_____

_____

Data from Method 2: _____

_____

_____

Work Form for an Electronic Resources Evaluation Project (*Continued*)

Data from Method 3: _____

_____

_____

VII. How will the library use the information gained from the evaluation project?

_____

_____

_____

VIII. How will the library disseminate the results of the study?

_____

_____

_____

IX. What methods are in place to ensure the study will be utilized by appropriate decision-makers?

_____

_____

_____

7 COPYRIGHT AND LICENSING ISSUES

The rapid growth of online and electronic resources has had and is continuing to have a profound impact on our society, our economy, and our libraries, and has even begun affecting our laws and commercial relationships. The development of increasingly powerful and sophisticated communications networks and associated information resources will continue to have a significant impact on intellectual property rights in the United States and around the world.

Copyright is a governmentally created right granted to the creators of literary works to protect their individual interest in their work through prohibiting the unauthorized printing, publishing, importing, or selling of multiple copies of a work; in essence, it functions as a protection from the unauthorized mass production and sale of a work. As such, copyright laws can be seen as a limitation on the dissemination of information. Libraries, on the other hand, have long been established to disseminate information on a mass basis, normally free-of-charge to the patron, essentially through the purchase and maintenance of authorized copies of works.

But with the development, in the last third of the 20th century, of fast and cheap photocopying, and as the physical limitations on making copies began to evaporate, a new problem for librarians arose. There might be only single copies made for a patron; however, the aggregate number of copies was potentially extremely high. In fact, the volume of copying became so great that copyright holders felt that their rights were being violated, and the rules of copyright had to adjust. Today, new forms of electronic resources have tremendously intensified the potential problems in this area for both libraries and copyright holders.

Presently, under the Copyright Term Extension Act of 1998, copyright protection in the United States is for the life of the author plus 70 years. The 1998 law also provides that works with so-called corporate authorship, and works that are anonymous or pseudonymous, are protected for 95 years after date of first publication or 120 years after creation, whichever comes first. Prior to the passage of the Copyright Term Extension Act, works published in 1923 would have passed into the public domain at the end of 1998; these works will now not be in the public domain until 2019. It should be noted that the copyright law also extends copyright protection to unpublished works as well as the published ones.

Under U.S. copyright laws, there are stated exceptions to the exclusive rights granted to copyright owners, and these exceptions are critical for libraries. These exceptions include:

- The right anyone possesses to use and reproduce materials in the public domain, for example, works created by U.S. federal government employees, works never copyrighted, or works that have passed beyond the copyright protection period.
- Fair use of copyrighted materials for the purpose of research, teaching, journalism, criticism, or even parody.
- Certain archival preservation rights for libraries, that is, the right to photograph, archive, or otherwise copy, in order to protect or preserve the work.
- Copying for interlibrary loan for the use of another library's patrons.

Where to draw the line between creators' and users' rights has always presented lawmakers with a very complicated problem. Producers of works must be encouraged to risk creating something new and to make their work available in some form to the public; if their work risks becoming free for the asking, the author may be encouraged to keep it a secret—a major justification for the copyright laws. However, users of materials also have needs and they should enjoy certain rights that the copyright laws recognize.

Since the introduction of the copying machine, many librarians have had to become familiar with copyright law and its provisions regarding "hard" copies of works, and they are now accustomed to dealing with copyright issues in the delivery of information services. It might be relatively easy to consider that the same restrictions would apply to electronic materials except that their use is most often restricted through licensing agreements, which are really extensions not of copyright law, but of contract law.

The Internet and the Web did not introduce libraries to the concept of resource licensing. OCLC or Dialog or other online mainframe systems have for many years used network resource license agreements that libraries have had to sign, but CD-ROMs acquisitions, quickly followed by Internet/Web resources such as electronic journals and other full-text resources, have opened the proverbial Pandora's box of issues and problems for libraries in the area of copyright and licensing.

Many of the traditional fair use rights that libraries have enjoyed for print materials are no longer necessarily assured in the new electronic age of information. As time goes on, it would appear that contracts for the acquisition and utilization of electronic resources will become both increasingly more common and at the same time more complex. This is an area where librarians generally have been slow to react. Although it is instantly recognized that electronic products do not "behave" in the same way as a print resource, the corollary that electronic publishers will not want to and usually do not behave like print publishers is a concept that librarians have been slow to grasp.

More and more electronic vendors no longer sell their electronic products outright. Rather, they simply provide to libraries a mere license of the right to use their products, and the license may be revocable in certain events—a significant contrast to a permanent book acquisition, for instance. Today, dealing with licensing agreements has become unavoidable for acquisitions librarians. Moreover, managing and negotiating licensing agreements has become an enormous task for many libraries as the number of available databases rapidly increases, and the variety of licensing restrictions and special clauses applicable to them seem to be growing at an even more rapid rate.

The Digital Millennium Copyright Act, passed by Congress in 1998, contains a number of new restrictions in regard to electronic resources. The law now prohibits the "circumvention" of any effective "technological protection measure" (for example, bypassing a password or a form of encryption) used by a copyright holder to restrict access to its materials. It also prohibits the manufacture of any device, or the offering of any service, primarily designed to defeat such a protection measure. It should be noted that these prohibitions are presently deferred in order to give the Librarian of Congress (through the Copyright Office and in consultation with the U.S. Department of Commerce) time to conduct a rulemaking proceeding to determine whether the anticircumvention prohibitions will adversely affect information users' ability to make noninfringing uses of particular classes of copyrighted work. The investigation may result in a three-year waiver from the anticircumvention prohibition for one or more classes of copyrighted works. (The term "class" was deliberately left undefined but seems to be intended to be fairly narrow, for example, history texts, digital maps, and so on.)

PURCHASE VERSUS LICENSED RIGHT OF USE

When a library is acquiring any new electronic resources, a key issue to consider is whether the library will be actually purchasing the resource or only obtaining a right or license to use it. This distinction, which may sound inconsequential at first blush, is nevertheless extremely important regarding the fair use rights of the library purchaser, and regarding the library's long-term access to the material. From the beginning, the drafters of copyright laws have generally agreed that at least some kinds of copying should be permitted. Over the years in the United States, there developed the concept of "fair use," whereby a purchaser of, for example, a copyrighted book might lawfully copy without fee or restriction a few pages for personal use, copyright notwithstanding. The problem lies in defining what constitutes "fair" use. The U.S. copyright law codifies the fair use doctrine in general terms, referring to such permissible purposes or uses as criticism, comment, news reporting, teaching, scholarship, or research. The law also specifies four criteria to be considered in determining whether a particular instance of copying or other reproduction is in fact fair:

- The purpose and character of the use, including whether the use is of a commercial nature or is for nonprofit educational purposes.
- The nature of the copyrighted work.
- The amount and substantiality of the portion used in relation to the copyrighted work as a whole.
- The effect of the use upon the potential market for or value to the owner of the copyrighted work.

Looking at these factors, and depending on the circumstances, fair use might cover not only making a single copy but also multiple copies. For example, the statute specifically states that multiple copying for classroom use may fall within the category of fair use copying.

The current U.S. copyright law also recognizes a "first sale doctrine," which allows the purchaser of a legally produced copy of a copyrighted work, (for example, a book that has been purchased from the copyright holder, such as a publisher) the right to sell or loan that copy to others. But if the actual legal title to the work itself is still retained by the vendor (that is, if the work itself is not sold), the work is said to be licensed, and the purchaser obtains only a right to the use of the item, rather than the full bundle of rights that a purchaser ordinarily obtains when he buys a book. This means that, without a sale, copyright concepts such as fair use and first sale doctrine are simply not directly applicable.

These distinctions are very important in the typical library context. For instance, a licensed right of use does not automatically allow the library to do all the things it typically and traditionally has done with its library materials (such as loan, circulate, or even sell the work to others). In a licensing regime, what the library can legally do with the resource being obtained is strictly limited to those activities or uses that are specifically set forth in the contract or license document pursuant to which the library acquires the item. Therefore, the license document itself becomes a much more critical document than a typical purchase order, and in the case of libraries the terms of use contained in a license agreement become matters of such importance that they should always be carefully negotiated by the library with the vendor of the item whenever possible.

This distinction is particularly important for library purchases of computer software. Many, but not all, purchase agreements for computer software now allow the buyer to make a backup copy of the software in case the original is destroyed. If this element is not contained in the purchasing agreement, Section 117 of the Copyright Act actually authorizes such a backup if the software was purchased, but Section 117 of the copyright law does not apply to licensed software. If a library is not a purchaser of software, the library has no Section 117 rights; rather, it has only the rights set out in the licensing agreement.

ASPECTS OF LICENSING RESOURCES

When dealing with electronic products in libraries today, licensing agreements are a critical fact of life. Initially, when many libraries began ordering computer software and CD-ROMs, the so-called "shrink-wrap" licenses printed in small type on the envelopes containing the software were often simply ignored; many users thought the licenses were so one-sided as to be virtually unenforceable. However, most librarians have begun to realize that these provisions are indeed enforceable. Librarians are also having to deal with licenses for Web-accessed databases and journals, where they must sign a license agreement with a publisher or distributor before being able to access the resource at all. With this in mind, it is always advisable to inquire about the terms of the licensing agreement before ordering a product. Many publishers are quite willing to send the library an advance copy of the license agreement; the library can thus review the license to determine whether the intended use is indeed allowed. Some publishers, unfortunately, do not even mention the existence of a licensing agreement in their catalogs and brochures, and the contract is simply sent after the order is placed. It is thus possible for a product to be received and the invoice paid before the library even gets the contract and sees the conditions imposed on its usage of the product—a most unhappy situation.

Librarians entering into licensing agreements face four major challenges:

- Understanding the content.
- Determining the wording required for your institution.
- Negotiating areas of the contract that require negotiation.
- Identifying who should negotiate and sign the agreement.

CONSIDERATIONS IN LICENSE NEGOTIATION

Whatever rights the library may have to search, copy, and use the information contained in the resource are all set forth in the license agreement. Librarians today typically face one of two basic licensing concepts:

- Contracts for online services or access licenses (for example, Lexis-Nexis), usually manifested by a specific written contract signed by at least the licensee.
- Contracts governing the use of a licensor's software on the licensee's equipment or network (that is, software licenses). Agreement of the parties to the terms of such a contract usually is not evidenced by a signed contract but rather by a broken shrink-wrap package or a click-through "OK" initiated by the licensee installing the software, without which click the software cannot be installed.

Access licenses involve significant ongoing obligations not typically or necessarily involved with software licenses, such as the licensor's obligations to provide access or the licensee's continuing obligation to pay for services as received. Software licenses are not always viewed by librarians as being distinct from the ownership of the works involved, but they are not the same. With a license, the right to use the information is typically all you get. License agreements used by different vendors vary widely and are not standard and predictable, so it is important to read each license carefully and consider the following points.

- How does the vendor define "site" and "user"? For example, a site could be undesirably limited to a particular computer, a particular building, or a particular campus. A user could be a registered borrower for a public library, a faculty or staff member or a student for an academic library or school media center, an onsite user, anyone who comes into the library, or anyone who accesses the library via the Internet.
- Can off-site users obtain access to the electronic resource?
- If a library has multiple branches or has units or access nodes located on several campuses, does the license cover only the main branch/campus or are all of the locations appropriately provided for?

- Can users print, download, or copy from the resource? If so, is there a limit to the number of copies? Some licenses may specify the number of copies, and, if so, the library will be responsible for communicating these restrictions to its users.
- Is the library allowed to make copies of the electronic resource, or portions thereof, for interlibrary loan purposes?
- Will you have permanent rights to the information that is licensed in case a licensed database is subsequently canceled or removed by the publisher? Do you have the right to archive the material?
- Does the vendor's software contain electronic "self-help" or a "time bomb" or similar provision which, after a certain period of time, allows the vendor unilaterally to shut down the library's use of an application or resource either remotely by the vendor or automatically?
- Are you licensing material that is already in the public domain? Oftentimes expensive bundles of electronic resources include public domain material as a large portion of the licensed product.
- Does the license limit your ability to enhance the information, so long as content integrity is maintained, to make the resource more easily usable by the library's patrons (such as by adding annotations or links to other holdings)?
- What happens if there are unauthorized uses of the resource? A license agreement should not hold the licensee liable for unauthorized uses so long as the licensee has implemented reasonable and appropriate measures to notify its users of restrictions. If such uses occur, the licensor should be required to give the licensee notice of any suspected license violations and allow a reasonable time for the licensee to look into the matter and take corrective actions if appropriate.
- Does the license agreement hold the licensee harmless from any actions based on a claim that use of the resource in accordance with the license infringes any patent, copyright, or trademark or trade secret of any third party?
- How may you terminate the license? The contract should provide termination rights that are appropriate for each party.

CHOOSING A LICENSE NEGOTIATOR

Unfortunately, the acquisition of electronic products means that some-one in the library needs to be prepared to negotiate or conduct pre-liminary negotiations with the vendors. The following is a list of possible choices for the role of negotiator:

- Library Director
- Assistant Director
- Acquisitions Librarian
- Systems Librarian
- Counsel for the Library/University/Business

Some libraries use a combination of people and do not make a single individual responsible for all license negotiations. Often a designated individual from the library will work with the vendor to negotiate needed language and then refer the contract to the organization's at-torney for final wording and approval. In any event, it is important for everyone involved to learn the "legalese" of licensing and know what the required language may be for your library or institution. The library should also develop and follow baseline standards for what is acceptable for its licensing contracts. The librarian or other person designated for preliminary license negotiations should be prepared to reject offers and terminate negotiations if no reasonable solution is possible. Products that do not offer licensing contracts that can be made satisfactory for a particular library's clientele are simply not worth the cost of the license. What good is an electronic resource if you cannot effectively use it?

It is best not to abdicate responsibility to legal counsel for deciding whether to sign a particular license. The attorney will understand the legal ramifications and be able to explain them to you, but the attor-ney will not necessarily understand the ramifications of the license restrictions from a library user point of view. Librarians must stay involved in the process to ensure that licenses for electronic materials carry only those provisions that the library and its users can live with.

In general, it appears that licensing agreements are becoming a bit more favorable for library users—as librarians become more familiar with and adept at negotiating, and as publishers and vendors become more familiar with typical library needs and more comfortable with removing or modifying restrictions in their agreements to accommo-date those needs. At first, either the library market was deemed not to be the major market for particular electronic products, or vendors sim-ply did not conceive of how to write a license for the library market.

These initial problems are fortunately fast becoming obsolete with more and more electronic resource vendors catering to the library market.

LICENSING CONSIDERATIONS

All rights and permissions need to be completely described in a document provided by each publisher or vendor for each electronic product. Some publishers require subscribers to officially sign a license. In such a case, it is necessary to ensure that someone who has the authority to commit the organization to a contract is the individual who signs the contract. Few organizations will allow a collection development librarian or an acquisitions librarian to sign an official contract. Other publishers simply provide a document that describes the conditions and terms governing the use of the resource. Although electronic aggregators cannot sign contracts on your behalf, many will collect them and provide them for your review. They can also frequently assist you if it is necessary to negotiate terms in order to satisfy the requirements of your institution or governmental agency. It is vitally important for you to read and understand the requirements for each product, even when the agreement is a "shrink-wrap" or "click-through" license on a product downloaded from the Web.

Figure 7–1: Licensing and Negotiation Work Form

I.   Who will be responsible for negotiating the license?

_____

II.   How does the proposed license define both the "site" and an "authorized user"?

Site: _____

_____

Authorized User: _____

_____

III.   How does the library determine who its "authorized users" will be?

_____

_____

IV.   May off-site users obtain access to the electronic resource

        ☐ Yes   ☐ No

Under what conditions or restrictions?

_____

_____

_____

V.   Does the license allow users to   print? _____ Limitations:_____

                                       download? _____ Limitations:_____

                                            copy? _____ Limitations:_____

Can the library make a copy for ILL purposes? _____ Limitations:_____

Licensing and Negotiation Work Form (*Continued*)

VI.   Will the library have permanent access to the information if the license is subsequently cancelled or the resource removed by the publisher?

☐ Yes   ☐ No

What alternatives are available for access? _____

_____

Is there a commitment from the vendor to archive?

☐ Yes   ☐ No

If yes, what are the vendor's access policies? _____

_____

May the library archive the material?

☐ Yes   ☐ No

If yes, what restrictions apply? _____

_____

VII.   Are you proposing to license material that is already in the public domain?

☐ Yes   ☐ No

If so, where? _____

_____

VIII. What happens under the license if there are unauthorized uses made of the resource?

_____

_____

_____

_____

Licensing and Negotiation Work Form (*Continued*)

IX. Does the license agreement hold you the licensee harmless from any actions based on a claim that use of the resource in accordance with the license infringes any patent, copyright, trademark, or trade secrets of any third party?

☐ Yes   ☐ No

X. How may you terminate the license?

_____

_____

XI. How may the licensor terminate the license?

_____

_____

BEST PRACTICES

A number of organizations have put together useful standards for licensing agreements. These standards include:

- **Association of Research Libraries**
  "Licensing Electronic Resources: Strategic and Practical Considerations for Signing Electronic Information Delivery Agreements." *http://arl.cni.org/scomm/licensing/licbooklet.html*
  Contains major considerations and good approaches to licensing electronic resources.

- **Columbia University Libraries**
  "Electronic Resource Coordinator Draft License Agreement Checklist." *www.columbia.edu/cu/libraries/inside/ner/license-checklist.html*
  Contains a checklist of 17 items that cover some of the most important rights and provisions to look for in a licensing agreement.

- **New England Law Library Consortium**
  "NELLCO Decision Criteria Worksheet for Electronic Acquisitions." *www.nellco.org/general/criteria.htm*
  Sets out a 31-question checklist geared toward law libraries, but the ideas and concepts behind the questions can easily be used and adapted by other types of libraries. This checklist covers much more than simply licensing issues.

- **University of California Libraries. Collection Development Committee**
  "Principles for Acquiring and Licensing Information in Digital Formats." *www.sunsite.berkeley.edu/Info/principles.html*
  Guides librarians in developing and reviewing proposals to/from, and in negotiating contracts with, providers of information in various digital formats.

- **University of Texas System**
  "Software and Database License Agreement Checklist." *www.utsystem.edu/OGC/intellectualproperty/dbckfrm1.htm*
  Covers eight major areas of concern, and guides librarians through a typical analysis of a licensing contract.

- **Yale University**
  "Licensing Digital Information: A Resource for Librarians."
  www.library.yale.edu/~llicense/index.shtml
  Presents a collection of materials with the purpose of providing librarians with a better understanding of the issues raised by licensing agreements in the digital age.

MANAGING LICENSES

Many libraries today have hundreds of licensing agreements for their various electronic products, ranging from computer programs that library staff use daily to the numerous CD-ROMs, databases, electronic books, and serials that are primarily for client use. In a large library, it is a certainty that not every staff member who uses a product will have been involved in negotiating and signing the agreement, but they should all be aware that they are still bound by that agreement. There is also an obligation for library staff to make licensing restrictions known to their library's users and to take reasonable steps to help them abide by the terms of the license. Since very few licensing agreements will contain exactly the same list of permitted and restricted uses, it is necessary for the librarians to create some system by which the licenses can be easily accessed when needed.

Some libraries are starting to build internal databases (more likely as not searchable Web-based databases) of all their existing licenses. When development of this approach appears appropriate, such a database should include provisions that adequately address the following questions:

- What constitutes an authorized user and use?
- What may constitute an unauthorized use? (For example, is interlibrary loan of the material permitted?)
- What manner of access (such as password or IP address) is allowed?
- What other special provisions of the license are important for librarians and/or users to know?

Such a database could also be used to track the negotiation process for specific products in order to alert library staff as to the expected availability of a resource. Proper management of licensed resources is critical because the license is a contract to which the library has agreed, and the library is legally bound to uphold its provisions. If the license for a particular resource does not allow interlibrary loans, then the

ILL staff must know this and abide by that restriction and, in addition, the catalog record for the item should reflect the restriction on interlibrary loans. However, although librarians must abide by the licenses, they should not always think of them as "straitjackets." Sometimes we tend to be more restrictive than is actually required, so a balance must be maintained between the rights of vendors and the rights of users.

AN IMPORTANT EMERGING COLLECTION DEVELOPMENT CONCERN IN THE LICENSING OF ELECTRONIC RESOURCES: UCITA

The Uniform Computer Information Transactions Act, or UCITA (originally prepared as an amendment to that portion of the Uniform Commercial Code governing sales transactions in most of the United States and formerly described as UCC2B) is a new uniform law approved and proposed for adoption by the states in July 1999 by the National Conference of Commissioners on Uniform State Laws (NCCUSL). UCITA deals with software and database licensing issues and basically covers contracts involving computer software, documentation, databases, e-books, Web sites, motion pictures, and sound recordings.

Librarians have traditionally focused their attention on the U.S. Congress and the national copyright laws when their concerns turned to matters of intellectual property and the use of copyrighted materials, but now this focus must be shifted to the state level, because the decisions made in each state legislature as to whether or not to enact UCITA will have an important impact on how libraries may continue to provide access to electronic resources for their patrons.

The ins and outs of contract law are already becoming more relevant to librarians as almost all libraries now regularly sign license agreements for online databases, software, and other types of information in digital format. With the passage of UCITA by various state legislatures, contractual licensing of electronic resources will become increasingly important in those states. But the ability of the individual library to negotiate favorable terms for its users as the library acquires electronic resources may be weakened by UCITA as vendors will, no doubt, attempt to create a "one size fits all" environment that may, in reality and from the library's point of view, be a "one size fits none" regime as libraries may find vendors more and more unwilling to negotiate acceptable licensing terms.

A proposed uniform law such as UCITA must be adopted by a state legislature before it becomes the law in that particular state. Since UCITA's proposal was unusually controversial (its supporters could not get it proposed as an addition to the otherwise universally adopted Uniform Commercial Code), there was some hope in the library community that UCITA would die on the vine. But with the passage of UCITA in Virginia, the first state to do so, by the General Assembly and its signing by the governor of Virginia on March 14, 2000, and UCITA's passage shortly thereafter in Maryland, it appears that librarians who license and then make available to their clients electronic resources of any kind will soon have yet another field in which they must become knowledgeable. While Virginia was the first state to pass UCITA, Maryland will be the first to make it effective, that is, as of October 1, 2000 (UCITA will become effective in Virginia on July 1, 2001). It is expected that UCITA, or something substantially similar, will be introduced in and actively considered for adoption by most other state legislatures in the United States over the next few years.

UCITA is an attempt to bring state laws into conformity as they relate to software licensing and covers software, multimedia interactive materials, data and databases, as well as Internet and other online information, and offers a number of additional protections for producers of electronic resources that some (but not all) of the major software vendors and publishers have long felt to be necessary. Important from the librarian's point of view, UCITA will allow vendors legally to engage in "electronic self-help," that is, to disable their licensed software remotely or automatically (a practice sometimes referred to as inserting a "time bomb") in order to "repossess" their electronic products if they are not renewed or are used in a manner not necessarily to the licensor's liking. UCITA also makes so-called shrink-wrap and click-through (mass market licenses) licensing provisions more easily enforceable, prevents vendor-unauthorized transfers from one end-user to another, makes illegal most reverse engineering of software, and allows vendors to actually disclaim their warranties in certain situations.

Another important concern for librarians is that UCITA permits so-called nondisclosure clauses to be used to block reviews of the materials without permission from the vendor, thereby removing a major tool—the impartial review—which librarians customarily use when selecting materials to add to their library's collection.

In addition, UCITA allows provisions in license agreements prohibiting transfers without a further license or authorization, effectively eliminating the buyer's traditional rights under the first-sale doctrine, a doctrine crucial to how libraries currently offer most of their services. First-sale allows for the heart and soul of most libraries—the right to circulate their purchased materials. Under first-sale, the buyer of a legally made and legally acquired copy of a work has the essentially unrestricted right to lend, sell, display, or otherwise make use of that copy of the work; the copyright holder no longer has rights over that particular copy of the work. The buyer does not have the right to copy the work but does have complete rights over the physical copy that has been lawfully purchased.

Effective revocation through UCITA of first-sale rights in regard to electronic resources would mean that libraries could no longer assume that they can legally circulate computer software or CD-ROMs or DVDs to library users, if provisions in the license agreement in fact prohibit those activities. There is further concern that under UCITA a license agreement could limit any right that a library currently has under copyright law to make archival copies, and that expiration of a license would always terminate the library's access to the information.

Some legal experts note that passage of UCITA in all states may not be necessary for it to become effective nationwide. For example, many large software vendors and publishers are located in Virginia, and with UCITA's enactment in Virginia, its effects may be felt in states that have not passed UCITA through licensing contract provisions specifying the law of Virginia as being applicable to the license in question. If these "choice of law" provisions become common and are ultimately upheld by the courts, many vendors and publishers could simply establish a presence in Virginia or Maryland (and any other state that adopts UCITA) in order to take advantage nationwide of the additional protections offered them by UCITA. It should be noted that Iowa has recently passed legislation intended to prevent its citizens from being affected in this manner by UCITA, that is, making voidable in Iowa any contract provision that attempts to require the application of UCITA to Iowa residents through a "choice of law" contract clause. (However, the Iowa legislature has also indicated it will consider adoption of UCITA in 2001.)

Librarians must also be concerned about UCITA in terms of current fair use rights in regard to copyrighted materials. The concept of fair use has been explicit in the U.S. copyright laws since the Copyright Act of 1976 (supplemented by the Classroom Copying Guides or CONTU Guidelines), but before that it had long been enshrined in "judge-made doctrine" in various court decisions in order to balance the rights of copyright holders with the rights of the users of copyrighted material. Thus, various types of copying of copyrighted material for research, education and for reviewing purposes have always been recognized as legitimate and legally permitted. The provisions of UCITA challenge these traditional fair use rights and thus the very heart of library services.

Naturally, UCITA has come in for a great deal of criticism since the NCCUSL proposed it. Common concerns are that it is imbalanced in favor of the publishers and vendors of computer information, that it upsets state-based consumer protection laws, and that it negatively affects the balance between copyright law in the protection of intellectual property rights and the basic interests of the public education and library communities. UCITA's emphasis on "freedom of contract" is generally seen as problematic in a library acquisitions context, particularly in light of the reality of the one-sided nature of most licensing contract negotiations, particularly in regard to relatively inexpensive or "mass market" computer software.

Fortunately, librarians have become alert to the introduction of UCITA. Professional library organizations such as the Association of Research Libraries, the American Library Association, the American Association of Law Librarians, the Medical Library Association, and the Special Libraries Association have come out against the adoption of UCITA, and many of their Web sites provide useful materials about UCITA and cogent arguments against its implementation. The American Library Association Web site contains a draft of a letter that can be sent to state legislators when UCITA is introduced in your state (*www.ala.org/washoff/sampleletter.html*), something that should be considered by every library professional.

Another Web site that provides up-to-date information about UCITA (from a coalition that includes organizations from the professional library community, such as the American Library Association, and organizations from the computer industry, such as the Computer & Communications Industry Association, as well as individual businesses, such as the Prudential Insurance Company of America, Walgreens, and Circuit City Stores, Inc., for example, that oppose UCITA) and how it is faring in the various state legislatures is **4 CITE** (For a Competitive Information and Technology Economy) at *www.4cite.org/ HotNews.htm*. The official Web site of the Uniform Law Commissioners contains the various drafts and the final version of UCITA, with comments and other related materials, and is available at *www.law.upenn.edu/bll/ulc/ulc_frame.htm*. (This site contains information about many uniform laws that are being considered on many different subjects, so scroll down the list and click on Uniform Computer Information Transactions Act.)

The implications of UCITA for electronic resource collection development are obvious. Preference for the acquisition of electronic materials enjoying both permanence and free use ability by patrons are obviously to be preferred, but if UCITA becomes the rule in the United States it will be incumbent for librarians in developing electronic collections to do all they can to ensure that the licensing agreements into which they enter provide as much flexibility to the library in this regard as possible.

CONCLUSION

"Fair use" as provided for in the U.S. copyright laws has come increasingly under attack in the digital environment. Most librarians tend to believe strongly that traditional fair use rights must be as strongly maintained with regard to electronic resources as with print publications, and few would argue with this ideal; meanwhile, however, electronic publishers and other holders of copyright in respect of materials otherwise available electronically see a significant distinction. They base the distinction on the essentially free transferability of limitless numbers of "perfect" electronic copies, unrestricted by the traditional print environment factors of copy quality degradation and the physical time and space restraints that manual copying typically imposed. Striking a balance between these competing interests is difficult, but librarians have to recognize that, increasingly, our purchase of and reliance upon electronic resources is moving us away from traditional, familiar copyright considerations into the dangerous and unfamiliar world of licensing and contract law.

Assuming that one accepts the premise that copyright laws are still important to ensure the advancement of knowledge through journals and other means of distribution, it is the licensing issues (that is, the application of statutory commercial contract law governing the relationships of particular parties to particular contracts, as opposed to the statutory law principles promulgated in respect of the relations between the producers and the users of copyrighted works generally) that may fast be becoming the most important legal overlay to the digital library environment, more important even than changes in copyright law. Although copyright law and the limitations imposed contractually through licensing both often share a goal of protecting intellectual property, there are important distinctions in how these two legal constructs accomplish their respective purposes, and librarians must become increasingly familiar with these distinctions.

8 PRESERVATION ISSUES

In the rush to convert to electronic products and media, the traditional role of every library in preserving and archiving information for its particular community of users should not be forgotten. Libraries' users have generally depended on their librarians not only to select, purchase, organize, and make available currently needed resources, but also, as an inherent corollary to these actions, to save and preserve information that may have lasting value. Traditional library preservation strategies have therefore long been established for **physical** objects, but these strategies do not always neatly transfer to the preservation of a **digital** object. This is so because, in the past, libraries have been mainly concerned with taking steps to preserve the physical artifact (or a photocopied or microfilmed facsimile of the physical artifact) that contains the specific information desired, rather than preserving the information itself.

It was traditionally assumed that, if a publication were printed on long-life, acid-free paper and if reasonable environmental conditions for its storage were maintained, access to the information could continue for an essentially indefinite period or at least for quite a long time. This was work that was often well done—the oldest printed Gutenberg Bibles still in existence remain readable today, if not exactly easily usable in the sense of unrestricted access to the original. It is only relatively recently in library history that the format of materials has, however, become problematic for the preservation for future use of the information contained in those formats.

Although libraries have always needed to take steps to de-select or weed their collections of unneeded, out-of-date, duplicative, or otherwise no longer useful books and serials, this process has almost always been accomplished (barring natural disasters, fires, or other accidents) through a conscious and usually carefully considered decision on the part of librarians. However, electronic products open up the unhappy specter of the unconscious discarding, in effect, of the information itself through the outdating and obsolescence of the resource medium itself. For instance, if you purchase a serial on CD-ROM today, how certain are you, or can you be, that you will be able to access the material contained in its issues in the year 2010, or even two years from now? If you purchase Web access to that same serial, what happens if you drop the subscription next year, or if the company that provides you with access is bought out by another vendor that subsequently changes its access policies in ways incompatible with your systems or policies, or provides continued access only at significantly increased cost? If you decide to preserve a Web site, do you also have to preserve all the links made from that page if it is to be truly useful? If so, where do you stop? These are not issues only for research libraries; they are matters of concern for every library.

IS DIGITIZED INFORMATION PRESERVED (OR PRESERVABLE) INFORMATION?

Although sometimes the layman may think of digital information as being potentially preserved for eternity, it is becoming clear that at the present this is certainly not the case. Electronic formats keep changing, and unless the information contained in the older formats is constantly being transferred to the newer mediums, it can and will likely quickly become lost. For example, locating today a new or refurbished $5\frac{1}{4}$-inch floppy drive (for which compatible disks were the predominant storage format for most microcomputer users a mere five years ago) in order to read documents stored in that format is already more and more difficult. For those who have data on the even older 8-inch diskettes, accessing and moving the information contained on them to a current format remains a doable proposition, but one that is both expensive and labor-intensive. Even as august a body as the National Archives finds itself constantly on the search for, or even attempting to build from scratch, some older piece of technology or equipment so that the Archives can transfer information from an obsolete format to a new one. It has become clear that the preservation of digital information requires both the financial wherewithal and a firm commitment to migrating data from one format or medium to another so as to ensure that the data can continue to be read.

But even when a document (or information) is kept in a "readable" format, you must also consider the durability of that format. At present the average life span of magnetic tape appears to be considerably less than that of most books, even those printed on acidic paper. Magnetic disk formats, while apparently somewhat better, have yet to meet the test of time, even assuming adequate protection from magnets, motors, and electric detection equipment; for optical disk formats, such as CD-ROMs, the life expectancies are apparently considerably longer, but there is no consensus on just how long, and there appear to be variations depending on the type of disk—estimates vary all the way from 10 to 100 years—but the life expectancies are still paltry when compared to the expected lives of most printed materials.

Hardware format challenges are not the only ones lurking out there; the library must also be concerned about the software used to generate the documents themselves. In 1989 the latest in word processing software included such now extinct, or nearly so, programs as WordStar and XyWrite. Can we be positive that ten years from now we will have the software available to read or convert a document produced using one of today's standard word processing programs? It is clear that when we move away from standard ASCII text to formatted, word-processed documents, we necessarily become very dependent on having available the proper software to read the document, suggesting perhaps the need for a standard for electronic archives.

Today, to preserve information, many archives often convert their materials to a format that is not software dependent or platform dependent format. Mainly such formats are pure ASCII texts, which are easy to save, but which lack the benefits of fancy fonts, boldfaced and italicized text, justification, and so on. Today, this approach seems the best, but it is an expensive one without any guaranties. After all, what future does ASCII have?

Another important consideration to keep in mind is that, unlike the situation with print materials, where good fortune often plays a crucial part in long-term preservation, there is no salvation in just doing nothing; electronic materials will be preserved and usable in the future only if positive action is taken on a current basis. In the past, many printed sources were saved by serendipity, that is, they just happened to survive on someone's bookshelf or in some library's otherwise unused storage area. In addition to depending on the lifespan of the material or medium on which they reside (magnetic tape, optical disk, and so forth), the "life" of electronic materials also depends on having available the hardware to run or play the physical medium on which the information is stored. As stated earlier, electronic information presently requires seemingly constant migration from one format to another in order to keep up with the advances that are being made in both software and hardware.

We can't ignore the problem. Generally, libraries are seen as having collections of items that are deemed to be of lasting importance rather than items of an ephemeral nature. Therefore, to meet this expectation libraries must be able to access permanent archives of information that are available only in electronic form. In searching for a solution, librarians are justifiably reluctant to depend on commercial vendors to archive their materials, and they must therefore make the necessary commitment to move with the technology so as not to be left with something like the equivalent of an 8-track audiotape cartridge archive. A March 1998 statement of the International Coalition of Library Consortia (ICLC) argues that libraries, if they are to meet their typical preservation and collection mandates, must be able to purchase or license information perpetually, and not just temporarily license the electronic information they collect, so that libraries will retain control over the preservation of the information contained in the media, and this control necessarily includes the right to make back-up copies. The problem is exacerbated when information is accessed only remotely, and the ICLC also argues that a provider should not be used unless there exists some form of guarantee as to the perpetual availability of the information.

WHO SHOULD ARCHIVE AN ELECTRONIC INFORMATION RESOURCE?

There are several possible answers to the question of who should archive electronic materials.

PUBLISHER OR VENDOR/AGGREGATOR

Many publishers do currently attempt to archive their electronic publications, but the problem seen by many in the library profession is that most such publishers make no commitment regarding the permanence of their archives. When it is no longer commercially profitable to do so, it appears unlikely that publishers will continue to make and maintain archives of their electronic materials. Librarians also worry that a publisher may go out of business or be sold to another company that decides that it is no longer in its financial interest to continue the archival arrangements of the first company. To make matters worse, even fewer publishers have indicated a commitment to moving their materials to current formats as needed for their preservation. Librarians in academic and research libraries strive to purchase materials for permanent retention, so preservation and archival issues are extremely important to them; depending on the publisher, however, the safeguards that may be in place will likely not be sufficient for a library's needs.

Some good approaches do exist. An example of a vendor approach to preservation is OCLC's FirstSearch Electronic Collections Online, which offers to subscribers perpetual access to its electronic resources.

THE LIBRARY ITSELF

Traditionally, libraries have always done their own archiving, whether through binding journal issues or in microfilming certain resources. It is conceivable that, given the permission of the publisher for licensed items, libraries could archive many of their electronic materials as well. However, the library must then make the same commitment to keeping materials in a current and usable format, and, if done in every library, these activities would certainly be expensively duplicative on numerous occasions. Librarians would doubtless feel the "safest" or most comfortable with this solution, but it is probably not a cost-effective approach to a general problem and it does not seem to be the method chosen by most libraries at this time. The one exception appears to be for materials produced locally, which many libraries do archive on the basis that they will likely be the "sole source" for these items in the future.

COOPERATIVE ARRANGEMENTS

As libraries have done with shared online cataloging for years, a cooperative arrangement could be worked out to preserve electronic resources, and this seems a most desirable approach. One suggestion currently making the rounds is that publishers could provide for a nonprofit organization, which would enjoy the right to archive and convey materials as needed and make particular titles and volumes available to libraries that held a valid subscription or had once held a subscription for the particular title and volume. A number of efforts are under way along these lines. For example, the Committee on Institutional Cooperation's Electronic Journal Collection is an effort by the major academic libraries in the United States both to archive and to offer access to freely available electronic journals. An additional example of a consortial approach by academic libraries is JSTOR, which provides for archiving of electronic journals for a fee.

WHO SHOULD BE CONCERNED WITH PRESERVATION ISSUES?

When reviewing the practical, how-we-did-it-well library literature dealing with electronic resources, it is obvious that a good many libraries have determined, whether consciously or by default, that preservation of electronic format materials may not be a matter for their concern. Preservation issues are simply not a part of their checklists of points to consider when purchasing or licensing an electronic resource. In some cases, it has been baldly stated that preservation issues were not of concern to that particular library when selecting materials. But it is clear that other libraries are obviously very concerned with such issues, even if they do not have answers for all the preservation issues that are necessarily raised.

This is an area where no library can be a self-sufficient island. Some type of cooperation and "unitary" concern is necessary if vendors and publishers are to make significant contributions to ensuring continued access to electronic materials. If the library community is deemed unconcerned, then the vendors and publishers obviously will not commit significant corporate dollars to ensure that their materials are in fact available in perpetuity. Also, libraries may need to follow the lead of a few cooperative efforts that have begun forming to work actively toward the preservation of electronic resources. Currently these efforts are mostly in the area of electronic serials, but that area of concern can be expected to widen in the near future.

Is this an issue only for research libraries? Although research libraries are naturally the ones most likely to be able and motivated to commit resources to cooperative preservation efforts, it is really a matter of concern for all libraries. Many smaller libraries currently rely on being able to borrow through interlibrary loan many specialized materials from a local academic or research library. What if that library that you have always depended on does not have hard-copy access to the material or, by the terms of a licensing agreement, cannot even loan you the material, much less print or copy any of it for your use? Preservation concerns involving electronic resources are properly the concern for all libraries and only by indicating that concern when you purchase or license materials can you help to ensure that the electronic materials will continue to be accessible.

CONCLUSION

Preservation concerns regarding electronic resources are far from being adequately resolved. For the foreseeable future, concerns are very real regarding continued hardware and software availability for reading the present generation of electronic materials. Access to licensed material involves both these issues and the legal right of future access to material that was previously licensed. We must ensure that the licenses that libraries sign today are not for limited access for a particular time period but that they allow for continued access to that same licensed material in the future. We must also have some protection from losing access to material when vendors are merged with larger companies or go out of business entirely.

To be secure in the knowledge of continued access in the future, cooperative arrangements between vendors and libraries are probably required. It would be naive in the extreme on the part of librarians to assume, once it is no longer profitable to maintain a resource, that the resource will somehow be maintained simply because future users might need access to it. Since for-profit businesses are indeed in business to turn a profit, cooperative arrangements in the nonprofit sector are probably required in order for perpetual access to be maintained. These kinds of arrangements, of course, will require the cooperation of vendors and publishers in order to allow libraries or special nonprofit organizations to preserve the materials while allowing others to access those materials.

9 CONCLUSION

THE SELECTION PROCESS

The proliferation over the past two decades and the public acceptance in the last few years of electronic information resources have brought about dramatic changes in libraries during the 1990s, and these changes, while having a significant impact on all parts of the typical library, have had a truly profound effect on the work of collection development librarians. For many years, the explosive growth of publishing and the decline (in real dollars) of library budgets have resulted in increased pressure on library selectors not only to find the best resources for the library's users but also to find those resources at the lowest possible price.

The proliferation and corresponding popularity of electronic resources have only increased that pressure, but, at the same time, technology has actually offered a way out of the problem through a more valid basis for "just-in-time" rather than "just-in-case" selection. The ability of a library to provide information not contained in physical form on its own shelves (whether through document delivery services, by online purchasing in general, and through telefacsimile, file transfers, or other forms of electronic delivery) means that any article or other resource needed by a client may be deliverable almost instantaneously, or at least within 24 to 72 hours—thereby significantly lessening the need for the many "just-in-case" purchases that most collection development librarians have traditionally felt were needed to meet their patron's anticipated or potential needs.

The importance of the selection process is reinforced by the traditional perception of many patrons that the library in some way vouches for the quality of the materials it collects, at least in the sense of the materials on the library's shelves being accurate representations of that which they purport to be. Much as we might from time to time hope to be able to disclaim connection with the content of every item in the materials made available in the library, the public does not usually see it that way, and this fact argues for even greater care in the selection of electronic resources, which are less easily controlled. Therefore, the growth of electronic resources will force librarians to become more collaborative in-house, with collection development librarians consulting with other librarians and specialists throughout the selection and implementation processes.

The expense of electronic resources is also bringing to the fore another type of collaboration—cooperative purchasing/licensing arrangements carried out through library consortia—that must be utilized if soaring costs are to be rationalized with budgets. Thus, we can safely say that building a library collection today must necessarily be much more of a team process than it typically was in the past (when selectors worked pretty much in isolation within their respective specified subject areas). Electronic resources, coupled with the growth in interdisciplinary studies and interests, necessitates changing the selection process in many libraries from an individual decision approach to a team decision basis.

INTEGRATION OF ELECTRONIC RESOURCES

Integrating electronic resources, and the hardware/software needs that accompany them, into the process of collection development presents both an exciting challenge and a multifaceted problem. Beyond the traditional tasks of selection exist numerous management issues concerning budgets and personnel, and the arenas of copyright and preservation, as well as the need for improved organization, including bibliographic control, for access to information.

In many ways, digital products have proven to be something of a mixed blessing for libraries, at least at this point in time. Some of the most difficult problems they present have to do with the budgetary problems they create, and this at a time when operating costs are increasing across the board. Electronic resources, with their concurrent hardware needs and training requirements, are now being demanded by users, yet most library budgets typically cannot even keep pace with the recent inflation in book/serial/database pricing. The combination of sudden public popularity and shrinking library budgets in "real dollars" creates a stressful situation for many librarians juggling to meet user demands and needs in the best way possible.

Collection development policies have always provided a focus for a library's collection and they are as essential for electronic resources as they have always been for traditional print materials. An integrated collection development policy that includes all types of resources is advocated as the best approach to the problem. Selection of electronic resources without the guidance of a collection development policy will usually lead to unfocused groupings of resources that may or may not fill the actual needs of the library's clients and that may or may not support the mission of the library as a whole. Because electronic resources are no longer frills to be treated almost as toys, but have become valid and necessary primary sources of information, they must be acquired in ways so as to fit into an overall collection plan.

Although, as we have seen, many of the basic traditional principles of collection development remain valid for electronic resources, methods of decision making and additional selection guidelines must be added to incorporate and reflect the differences between electronic and print resources. The old questions remain just as important in today's electronic environment as in the traditional print library:

- How should we select for collections and what do our users need?
- How do we make optimal use of limited budgets?
- How many serials and databases are sufficient and which particular ones are sufficient to meet our users' needs?
- How do we evaluate the existing collection and what can we do to determine its usefulness?

But selectors now often have to add to their choice of content the additional question of choice of format—print versus electronic, CD-ROM versus Web access, single-user access versus networked access for multiple users, individual subscription to a specific title versus a package of electronic titles from an aggregator. Another concern is how we determine what to purchase in this just-in-time information environment. Obviously, the library cannot wait for all materials to be requested before initiating access to them; but, on the other hand, it is considerably more difficult in today's environment to justify expenditures for items that are being or have been traditionally purchased only just in case they are needed.

Until very recently, the quality of access to information resources generally depended essentially on a user's physical proximity to a library and, of course, on the quality and quantity of the materials on that particular library's shelves. With users now demanding remote access to the library's electronic resources, more and more libraries are coming up with solutions to provide this service. These solutions have created additional problems that have to be considered and must be resolved, including which users should have access to which resources. Libraries must now also verify that their users are in fact persons who are permitted to have access to licensed, site-restricted, often Web-based information resources. Methods of vendor-allowed authentication may thus play an active role in the selection process, as many libraries do not wish to deal with resources that require the library to issue passwords to valid users; in many cases, even the method of IP source addressing does not meet the needs of the library's particular organization. Resources that use IP source addressing by requiring the library to set up a proxy server for remote users may also have to be taken into account.

Unfortunately, no single solution is universally correct and different approaches are required by different organizations in order to meet local end-user needs most effectively. Client authentication and authorization issues are quickly becoming complex issues for libraries as they move into networked electronic resources and as they join together in group purchases of information resources.

HANDLING THE STRESS OF CHANGE

It seems that change has become a constant in the library environment in any number of ways, and change always produces some level of stress in any organization. But it must be remembered that stress is not always bad, as it can be a consequence of good things as well as bad. Undertaking a new job or responsibility necessarily leads to stress, but hopefully it is a "good" kind of stress that helps the individual to learn and to grow in the job. In the library world, the introduction of technology has been related to many of those changes, and a relatively new, pithy term has even been devised for it—technostress.

There are a multitude of changes being driven by technology with which libraries today have to cope, and the increasing importance of electronic resources has forever changed the way libraries work. If we can find ways to fashion the electronic library out of the traditional print-based library, by using systematic procedures and policies, then libraries can continue to play in the future the valuable role they have always had; if not, users will, no doubt, find other means of obtaining what they need.

Librarians will also need to maintain a high degree of flexibility in this era of electronic resources. Old assumptions are constantly being challenged, and new ways of doing business are constantly being developed. As with early automation in the cataloging arena, organizational structures and reporting lines will need to change to accommodate team participation in the selection of electronic resources. Librarians may additionally find that their libraries are now members of multiple, and possibly overlapping and/or competing, consortia set up to purchase needed or desired electronic resources at the lowest possible cost. Likewise, vendors will begin to find themselves in commercial competition with, or sometimes in partnership with, their closest business rivals to provide needed electronic resource packages for their library customers. Indeed, online publications produced by libraries themselves may place librarians in the position of either working cooperatively or competitively with commercial vendors.

Librarians should not, however, feel threatened by the challenges presented by electronic and networked information resources. If you are just beginning to add electronic resources to your library's collection, the combination of learning new technologies and managing decisions about choices for format and methods of access may at first seem formidable to you. However, by doing a little homework and visiting other libraries that may be a little further along in the process, plus visiting exhibitors at library conferences, participating in demonstrations by vendors, and combing through the professional literature, you should be well prepared to make the leap into the provision of electronic resources.

Being prepared to work in teams and to cooperate with other libraries is probably also essential. Librarians will need to call upon all their technical, service, professional, and human resource skills if they are to thrive in this new and rapidly changing environment.

SELECTED BIBLIOGRAPHY

The following items have been selected and are presented to provide the reader with additional information on major topics covered in this work. This is by no means an exhaustive bibliography on the subject, but it should provide some good places to get started.

GENERAL WORKS

Atkinson, Ross. "The Acquisitions Librarians as Change Agents in the Transition to the Electronic Library." *Library Resources and Technical Services* 36 (January 1997): 7–20.

Billings, Harold. "Library Collections and Distance Information: New Models of Collection Development for the 21st Century." *Journal of Library Administration* 24, nos. 1/2 (1996): 3–17.

Buckland, Michael. "What Will Collection Developers Do?" *Information Technology and Libraries* 14 (September 1995): 155–159.

Crawford, Walt. *Being Analog: Creating Tomorrow's Libraries.* Chicago: American Library Association, 1999.

Demas, Samuel G. "What Will Collection Development Do?" *Collection Management* 22, nos. 3/4 (1998): 151–159.

Doyle, Greg. "Electronic Resources: Order Out of Chaos?" *OLA Quarterly* 4 (Fall 1998): 16–18.

Gorman, G. E., and Ruth H. Miller, eds. *Collection Development for the 21st Century: A Handbook for Librarians.* Westport, Conn.: Greenwood Press, 1997.

Gorman, Michael. "Ownership and Access: A New Idea of 'Collection.'" *College and Research Libraries News* 58 (July/August 1997): 498–499.

Harloe, Bart, and John M. Budd. "Collection Development and Scholarly Communication in the Era of Electronic Access." *Journal of Academic Librarianship* 20 (May 1994): 83–87.

Hitchingham, Eileen. "Collection Management in Light of Electronic Publishing." *Information Technology and Libraries* 15 (March 1996): 38–41.

Johnson, Peggy, and Bonnie MacEwan, eds. *Virtually Yours: Models for Managing Electronic Resources and Services.* Chicago: American Library Association, 1999.

Kanazawa, Midori. "Organization Theory and Collection Management in Libraries." *Collection Management* 14, nos. 1/2 (1991): 43–57.

Kovacs, Diane. *Building Electronic Library Collections.* New York: Neal-Schuman, 2000.

Lancaster, F. W. "Collection Development in the Year 2025." In *Recruiting, Educating, and Training Librarians for Collection Development*, ed. Peggy Johnson and Sheila S. Intner, 215–229. Westport, Conn.: Greenwood Press, 1994.

Mouw, James. "Changing Roles in the Electronic Age—The Library Perspective." *Library Acquisitions: Practice and Theory* 22, no. 1 (1998): 15–21.

Norman, O. Gene. "The Impact of Electronic Information Sources on Collection Development: A Survey of Current Practice." *Library Hi Tech* 15, nos. 1/2 (1997): 123–132.

Rowley, Gordon, and William K. Black "Consequences of Change: The Evolution of Collection Development." *Collection Building* 15, no. 2 (1996): 22–30.

Sankowski, Andrew. "Internet: Its Impact on Collection Development and the Curriculum." *Catholic Library World* 67 (March 1997): 16–18.

Schmidt, Karen A., ed. *Understanding the Business of Library Acquisitions*. 2d ed. Chicago: American Library Association, 1999.

Stolt, W. "Managing Electronic Resources: Public Service Considerations in a Technology Environment." *Collection Management* 21, no. 1 (1996): 17–28.

Stephens, Annabel L. *Public Library Collection Development in the Information Age*. New York: Haworth Press, 1998. Copublished as *The Acquisitions Librarian* 20, 1998.

COLLECTION DEVELOPMENT POLICIES

Davis, Denise M. "Designing a Collection Development Plan for Sailor.SM" *Collection Building* 14, no. 4 (1995): 29–33.

Demas, Samuel G., Peter McDonald, and Gregory Lawrence. "The Internet and Collection Development: Mainstreaming Selection of Internet Resources." *Library Resources and Technical Services* 39 (July 1995): 275–290.

Ferguson, Anthony W. "Interesting Problems Encountered on My Way to Writing an Electronic Information Selection Development Statement." *Against the Grain* 7 (April 1995): 16, 18–19, 90.

Hazen, Dan C. "Collection Development Policies in the Information Age." *College and Research Libraries* 56 (January 1995): 29–31.

Vogel, Kristin D. "Integrating Electronic Resources into Collection Development Policies." *Collection Management* 2, no. 2 (1996): 65–76.

White, Gary, and Gregory Crawford. "Developing an Electronic Resources Collection Development Policy." *Collection Building* 16, no. 2 (1997): 53–57.

COPYRIGHT AND LICENSING

Allen, Barbara McFadden. "Negotiating Digital Information System Licenses without Losing Your Shirt or Your Soul." *Journal of Library Administration* 24, no. 4 (1997): 15–23.

Bielefield, Arlene, and Lawrence Cheeseman. *Interpreting and Negotiating Licensing Agreements.* New York: Neal-Schuman, 1999.

Carson, Bryan. "Legally Speaking." *Against the Grain* 11, (December 1999/January 2000): 54–58

Davis, Trisha L. "License Agreements in Lieu of Copyright: Are We Signing Away Our Rights?" *Library Acquisitions: Practice and Theory* 21, no. 1 (1997): 19–27.

Okerson, Ann. "The LIBLICENSE Project and How It Grows." *D-Lib Magazine* 5 (September 1999): 8 pp. Available: *www.dlib.org/dlib/september99/okerson/09okerson.html.*

Webb, John. "Managing Licensed Networked Resources in a University Library." *Information Technology and Libraries* 17 (December 1998): 198–206.

ELECTRONIC JOURNALS

Ashcroft, Linda, and Colin Langdon. "Electronic Journals and University Library Collections." *Collection Building* 18, no. 3 (1999): 105–113.

Barnes, John H. "One Giant Leap, One Small Step: Continuing the Migration to Electronic Journals." *Library Trends* 45 (Winter 1997): 404–415.

Chadwell, Faye A., and Sara Brownmiller. "Heads Up: Confronting the Selection and Access Issues of Electronic Journals." *The Acquisitions Librarian* 21 (1999): 21–35.

Cochenour, Donnice. "CICNet's Electronic Journal Collection." *Serials Review* 22 (Spring 1996): 63–69.

Ellis, Kathryn D. "Acquiring Electronic Journals." *The Acquisitions Librarian* 21 (1999): 5–19.

Harter, Stephen P. "Accessing Electronic Journals and Other E-Publications: An Empirical Study." *College and Research Libraries* 57 (September 1996): 440–456.

Nisonger, Thomas E. "Electronic Journal Collection Management Issues." *Collection Building* 16, no. 2 (1997): 58–65.

EVALUATION AND ASSESSMENT

Bertot, John Carlo, and Charles R. McClure. "Measuring Electronic Services in Public Libraries." *Public Libraries* 37 (May/June 1998): 176–180.

Cooke, Alison. *Neal-Schuman Authoritative Guide to Evaluating Information on the Internet.* New York: Neal-Schuman, 1999.

International Coalition of Library Consortia. "Guidelines for Statistical Measures of Usage of Web-Based Indexed, Abstracted, and Full Text Resources." *Information Techonology and Libraries* 17 (December 1998): 219–221.

Kirkwood, Hal P. "Beyond Evaluation: A Model for Cooperative Evaluation of Internet Resources." *Online* 22 (July/August 1998): 66–68.

Svenningsen, Karen. "An Evaluation Model for Electronic Resources Utilizing Cost Analysis." *The Bottom Line: Managing Library Finances* 11 (1998): 18–23

ORGANIZATION AND ACCESS

Baker, Gayle, and Flora Shrode. "A Heuristic Approach to Selecting Delivery Mechanisms for Electronic Resources in Academic Libraries." *Journal of Library Administration* 26, nos. 3/4 (1999): 153–167.

Dempsey, Lorcan, and Rachel Heery. "Metadata: A Current View of Practice and Issues." *The Journal of Documentation* 54 (March 1998): 145–172.

Glenn, Ariel, and David Millman. "Access Management of Web-Based Services." *D-Lib Magazine* (September 1998). Available: *www.dlib.org/dlib/September98/millman/09millman.html.*

Goerwitz, Richard. "Pass-Through Proxying as a Solution to the Off-Site Web-Access Problem." *D-Lib Magazine* (June 1998). Available: *www.dlib.org/dlib/June98/stg/06goerwitz.html*.

Martin, Susan K. "Organizing Collections within the Internet: A Vision for Access." *Journal of Academic Librarianship* 22 (July 1996): 291–292.

Oder, Norman. "Cataloging the Net: Can We Do It?" *Library Journal* 123 (October 1, 1998): 47–51.

Porter, G. Margaret, and Laura Bayard. "Including Web Sites in the Online Catalog: Implications for Cataloging, Collection Development, and Access." *Journal of Academic Librarianship* 25 (September 1999): 390–394.

Simpson, Pamela, and Robert S. Seeds. "Electronic Journals in the Online Catalog: Selection and Bibliographic Control." *Library Resources and Technical Services* 42 (April 1998): 126–132.

PRESERVATION

Brichford, Maynard, and William Maher. "Archival Issues in Network Electronic Publications." *Library Trends* 43 (Spring 1995): 701–712.

Butler, Meredith A. "Issues and Challenges of Archiving and Storing Digital Information: Preserving the Past for Future Scholars." *Journal of Library Administration* 24, no. 4 (1997): 61–79.

Hunter, Gregory S. *Preserving Digital Information.* New York: Neal-Schuman, 2000.

Lynn, M. Stuart. "Digital Preservation and Access: Liberals and Conservatives." *Collection Management* 22, nos. 3/4 (1998): 55–63.

Smith, Abby. "Why Digitize?" Washington, D.C.: Council of Library Resources, 1999.

SELECTION

Caywood, Carolyn. "Library Selection Criteria for WWW Resources." Last revised December 1999. Available: *www6.pilot.infi.net/~carolyn/criteria.html*.

Clyde, Laurel A. "Evaluating and Selecting Internet Resources." *Emergency Librarian* 25 (March/April 1998): 32–34.

Davis, Trisha L. "The Evolution of Selection Activities for Electronic Resources." *Library Trends* 45 (Winter 1997): 391–403.

International Coalition of Library Consortia. "Statement of Current Perspective and Preferred Practices for the Selection and Purchase of Electronic Information." *Information Technology and Libraries* 17 (March 1998): 45–50.

Johnson, Peggy. "Selecting Electronic Resources: Developing a Local Decision-Making Matrix." *Cataloging and Classification Quarterly* 22, nos. 3/4 (1996): 9–24.

McGinnis, Suzan, and Jan H. Kemp. "The Electronic Resources Group: Using the Cross-Functional Team Approach to the Challenge of Acquiring Electronic Resources." *Library Acquisitions: Practice and Theory* 22, no. 3 (1998): 295–301.

Persons, Nancy A. "Collection Development in an Era of Full-Text and 'Package Deals.'" *Library Acquisitions: Practice and Theory* 22, no. 1 (1998): 59–62.

Pratt, Gregory F., Patrick Flannery, and Cassandra L. D. Perkins. "Guidelines for Internet Resource Selection." *College and Research Libraries News* 57 (March 1996): 134–135.

Walters, William H., Samuel G. Demas, Linda Stewart, and Jennifer Weintraub. "Guidelines for Collecting Aggregations of Web Resources." *Information Technology and Libraries* 17 (September 1998): 157–160.

INDEX

ABOUT THE AUTHOR

Vicki L. Gregory received an M.A. in History and an M.L.S. in Library Service from the University of Alabama and her Ph.D. in Communication, Library, and Information Studies from Rutgers University. She is currently Professor in and Director of the School of Library and Information Science at the University of South Florida in Tampa where she teaches courses in the areas of library networks, collection development, library automation, and technical services. Prior to beginning her library education career, she was the Head of Systems and Operations at the Auburn University at Montgomery Library.

She is the author of numerous articles and is an active member of the Special Library Association, the American Society for Information Science, the American Library Association, the American Association for Higher Education, the Association for Library and Information Science Education, the Southeastern Library Association, and both the Florida and Alabama Library Associations.